KW-483-173

How London Works

WITHDRAWN FROM STOCK

Department for Work & Pensions
Information Services

WITHDRAWN FROM STOCK

492765

AOI | Date:
Stelves | 20·10·03
Class:
331·12 HOW

WITHDRAWN FROM STOCK

How London Works

Simon Ellis
Amer Hirmis
Mark Spilsbury

KOGAN
PAGE

Publisher's note
Every possible effort has been made to ensure that the information contained in this book is accurate at the time of going to press, and the publishers and authors cannot accept responsibility for any errors or omissions, however caused. No responsibility for loss or damage occasioned to any person acting, or refraining from action, as a result of the material in this publication can be accepted by the editor, the publisher or any of the authors.

First published in 2002

Apart from any fair dealing for the purposes of research or private study, or criticism or review, as permitted under the Copyright, Designs and Patents Act, 1988, this publication may only be reproduced, stored or transmitted, in any form, or by any means, with the prior permission in writing of the publisher, or in the case of reprographic reproduction in accordance with the terms of licences issued by the Copyright Licensing Agency. Enquiries concerning reproduction outside those terms should be sent to the publishers at the undermentioned address:

Kogan Page Ltd
120 Pentonville Road
London N1 9JN
www.kogan-page.co.uk

© Simon Ellis, Amer Hirmis, Mark Spilsbury 2002

British Library Cataloguing in Publication Data

A CIP record for this book is available from the British Library

ISBN 0 7494 3784 7

Typeset by Saxon Graphics Ltd, Derby
Printed and bound in Great Britain by Biddles Ltd, Guildford and King's Lynn

Contents

Contents

Contents

List of Figures

List of figures

List of Tables

Acknowledgements

The research carried out by the London Skills Forecasting Unit (LSFU) between 1998 and 2001 relied on a wide range of sponsoring institutions and researchers. The LSFU reports that form the basis for this book were thus the product of a wide range of different people who cannot all be mentioned here.

The vast majority of funding for the studies came from the seven London Training and Enterprise Councils (TECs). Additional funding came from the London Development Agency, the regional office of the Employment Service, the London Development Partnership, the Skills Development Fund and the European Social Fund. Particular mention must be made of Judith Rutherford, who, as director of the London TEC Council, named the Unit and encouraged its development in every way.

Among the many scholars and researchers who contributed to the work of the Unit and whose thought is manifest in the following chapters are: Chris Hasluck, University of Warwick; Len Shackleton and Peter Urwin, University of Westminster Business School; Philip Roe, Prism Research; staff at BMG; Paul Owen and Kate Oakley; Mike Townsend; Mark Hepworth, Andrew Jones and John Fisher, Local Futures Group; Michele Harrison, The Henley Centre; Hilary Metcalf, National Institute for Economic and Social Research; and Judith Watson. Similarly, Professor Ian Gordon has been unstinting in his help with all aspects of the Unit's work.

The division of labour that has gone into this book is as follows: Simon Ellis wrote the Introduction and Chapters 1, 6 and 7; Amer Hirmis wrote Chapters 2 and 3; and Mark Spilsbury wrote Chapters 4 and 5. However, each of the authors has contributed his comments on the whole book. Simon Ellis has had overall editorial responsibility, although the authors share collective responsibility for any errors.

Finally, the following have contributed to the work of the LSFU as members of its research staff: Richard Cameron, Trevor Carr, Paul Ellis, Patrick McVeigh and Besiro Siraje. Their contribution is also gratefully acknowledged.

Simon Ellis
Head of the London Skills Forecasting Unit
September 2001

Introduction

It is impossible to describe the economy of the world's greatest cities, to capture the colour of Brick Lane, the buzz of the City, or the crowds of shoppers along Oxford Street. How is it possible to put the impact of the world's largest carnival at Notting Hill into figures? One of the mysteries of cities is how they fit together as a system, how international businesses and residential areas seem to move together, in conflict or cooperation, to take the whole forward into the future.

How London Works is a first attempt, for the non-expert reader, to set out some of the longer-term economic forces that have shaped and will continue to shape London in the foreseeable future. It tries to set out as it were the 'rules of the game' by which London operates. Sometimes it takes a global perspective, sometimes a local view within London, but always it tries to maintain a strategic long-term view to identify the broader economic forces.

What this book is and is not about

How London Works is a general introduction to the London economy, written by practitioners. It is purposely not filled with complicated formulae and does not rest on a particular theory or model of the London economy. It is a pragmatic book that aims to set out the main structures involved in the London labour market, indicating where the main centres of the region are located, what the growth industries are and why they are there.

The primary concern of the book is the economy of London and the part played in its growth by skills and training. It sets out to explain just that to people who work or live in London, and those with an interest in and commitment to the capital. It explains some of the main features of the London economy that determine who gets jobs in London and who doesn't. It explains why London has developed strengths in certain industries and certain parts of the capital. It explains why patterns of industry and employment changed in the recent past, and it suggests how they may change in the future. The terrorist attacks in the United States on 11 September 2001 have added an unanticipated degree of uncertainty to this assessment, but many of the economic forces set out here are long-term issues that are not easily deflected by the short-term shocks, however devastating and appalling they may be.

Explaining the working of a city can be extremely complicated. Some of the contributory factors determining location, structure and economic change include:

- entrepreneurship;
- existing clusters of industry;
- skills and training;
- education;
- tourism;
- governance and government;
- housing;
- cultural groupings and exchanges;
- religion;
- social grouping;
- physical environment;
- transportation and communications.

Although each of these factors will be mentioned in this book, some are much more central to our discussion than others. Indeed, some would be a matter for specialist treatises in their own right – for example, transport is a major issue for London, but requires a considerable amount of specialist knowledge that lies beyond the scope of this book.

It would be impossible to write about London and its economy without discussing the wide range of different social groups and neighbourhoods in the city. One of the exciting aspects of living and working in London is the great variety of people that one meets. However, this book is not concerned with London society, but with the London economy.

The physical environment is a major factor in London's economic success and thus one chapter of this work is devoted to economic geography. However, this is not a book about land-use planning and we do not consider issues such as the supply of land for industrial and/or office use in great detail. Similarly, although the difficulties of London's housing supply are discussed in Chapter 4, this work is not the place for a detailed analysis of how different social groups should be housed, or what public policy on this matter should be.

The economy is notorious for its unpredictability. Economists consider that a business cycle involves unemployment or growth depending on where you are – at the trough or peak. At the time of writing there is a feeling of foreboding. The United States is believed to be in recession and Europe waits to see whether it will follow. There is considerable debate in the United Kingdom as to whether we should join the European Single Currency – the euro. The object of this book is to set out the long-term forces that have moulded London's economy, rather than short-term traumatic shocks that may have a temporary distorting effect. Thus, Chapter 1 looks at the long-term decline of manufacturing in London, and explains terms such as the 'information' or 'new' economy, but does not cover the oil crisis of the early 1970s. Indeed, many major shocks that at the time seemed to be fundamental have, in hindsight, proved to be of short duration, such as the financial crises resulting from the collapse of stock markets in South East Asia in the second half of the 1990s.

Instead, *How London Works* aims to set out some of the economic forces that have constrained London's development, determining the way that the economy functions, sometimes over centuries. For example, London has always had a major function as a 'gateway'. Where originally that gateway function was exercised through its ports, now it operates through its airports and the Channel Tunnel. The development of the gateway function at Heathrow has led to the growth of the M4 corridor of high-tech industry. The current prosperity of London has led to increasing numbers of international migrants through airports and the Channel Tunnel.

London is a 'world city' and the international aspects of its economy are explored in Chapter 3. This is carried out from a London perspective. We are interested in London in a global context rather than the global economy. We point out where London's economy links into these global structures. A particular emphasis is placed on international competitiveness – which industries in which other cities compete with London, and how London may be vulnerable to global economic forces.

London is the capital of the United Kingdom, the seat of national government, with 33 local administrations and a new regional government. Everyone who works in London is conscious of its governmental role. International and national companies establish their headquarters in London in order to be close to government and its policy-making operations. Government at all its levels is again, however, not the subject of this book.

Much of what is discussed in *How London Works* has been shaped by European, national and local policy, but the role of this book is to look at the underlying structures within London's economy. It may identify problems, but it is not a polemical text to make recommendations about how such problems might be resolved through local or regional policy. The current institutional framework for skills and economic development in London has only been in place for 2000/1, including the Greater London Authority, the London Development Agency, the Learning and Skills Councils, and Business Link for London. Their strategies and mode of operation were still emerging at the time when this book was written. It would be rash to be judgmental while it is not clear what their priorities will be and how they will be achieved.

Chapters 4 through 6 are more concerned with the labour market for people who live and work in London than the economic conditions surrounding businesses. Chapter 4 discusses the factors that lead people to move into, around and out of London looking for housing and jobs. It shows how people live inside or outside London depending on their age and at what level commuters compete for jobs with residents. Chapter 5 addresses the central concerns of the London Skills Forecasting Unit (LSFU) – skills and training. It sets out the difference between skills and qualifications and how they both relate to job opportunities.

Chapter 6 covers the great problem of unemployment. It attempts to explain why it is such a persistent problem in certain areas of London. It explains how unemployment relates to broader concepts of social disadvantage – 'deprivation' and 'social exclusion'. This book is, however, still concerned with the economic aspects of these problems and not with the admittedly appalling consequences of long-term unemployment on social relations and the broader community.

Chapter 7 looks to the future, given the major dimensions of change and structural forces set out in the earlier chapters.

London Skills Forecasting Unit

The London Skills Forecasting Unit (LSFU) was founded by the London TEC Council in 1998. The Training and Enterprise Councils (TECs) were established by government in the early 1990s to examine local skill requirements and manage the delivery of suitable training programmes. All TECs had some research function to help determine the skill requirements. The seven London TECs remitted the London TEC Council to coordinate their research across London.

Much TEC research was based on surveys of employers and households. Such surveys are retrospective. The data must be collected, analysed, and the policy implications assessed. As a result, policies may be changed, which may lead to changes in training curricula, which must be linked with changes to qualifications. Finally, students must undertake the training and graduate. However, by the time all this has been achieved, the economy has moved on, creating new requirements! The LSFU aimed to look into the future rather than the current situation, to establish training requirements that would help keep London and London's workers ahead of the game with skills that would make them competitive in a changing world.

This approach entailed understanding the underlying forces of the London economy and how skill development contributed to them. Between its foundation in 1998 and the abolition of the TECs in April 2001, the LSFU published some 15 reports on skills and the London economy. Every year, the LSFU undertook the largest surveys of London's economy, including 5,000 employers and 14,000 workers. Sector studies were published on construction, retail and creative industries.

How London Works is a summary of the understanding of the London economy gained during this time, and is a tribute to the many people who contributed work to the Unit – staff of the London TEC Council, staff of London TECs, and consultants who worked on our research projects.

Since April 2001, the Unit has been run by a management board that includes the London Development Agency, Business Link for London, the Regional Office of the Employment Service, and the five London Local Learning and Skills Councils. The content of this book represents work undertaken before these new management arrangements were put in place.

This book has been written by Simon Ellis, Head of the LSFU, Amer Hirmis of Londonomics Ltd and Mark Spilsbury of Spilsbury Research – two consultants who played a large part in the work of the Unit from 1998 until 2001. The authors collectively are ultimately responsible for any errors the book may contain. The opinions contained in the work are solely those of the authors and do not represent those of their past or current employers or sponsors.

1
Structure and Change in the London Economy

People know that the City of London is the one of the world's top finance centres and that Heathrow is the world's busiest airport. People also know that London is a leading centre for the creative industries – a major tourism centre, with leading fashion houses, advertising agencies, publishers and music producers. Many people do not know, however, how these industries relate to one another. Indeed, one school of thought sees the financial centre of the City as virtually independent of all other industrial sectors.

Table 1.1 shows how London consistently outperforms in terms of the overall level of production per work place. When this is assessed per resident (ie omitting commuters), London ends up with a lower per capita GDP, but still outperforms all other regions of the United Kingdom.

The second theme of this chapter is industrial change. Between the mid-1970s and the mid-1990s, London changed from being a centre of manufacturing to being a centre for service industry. This is a reflection not only of the decline of manufacturing, but also of the way in which new industries are emerging in the 'information economy'.

Table 1.1 GDP per work place 1990–1998, indexed to United Kingdom

	1989	1990	1991	1992	1993	1994	1995	1996	1997	1998	1999
London	147.5	146.5	146.2	146.3	145.9	145.5	143.6	142.0	144.5	148.0	146.3
South East	102.7	103.7	103.4	103.8	104.9	105.3	104.4	107.1	108.8	109.4	110.2
U.K.	100	100	100	100	100	100	100	100	100	100	100

Source: DTI Regional Competitiveness Indicators, March 2001

A good starting point for discussion is the changing pattern of employment in London over the past 20 years (Table 1.2). Table 1.2 shows that the most dramatic change took place between 1981 and 1991. In 1981, employment in London was relatively evenly distributed between half a dozen key sectors. More people were employed in manufacturing than in financial and business services. Distribution (ie wholesale and retail trading), hotels and catering were the second largest source of employment after education, health and other services. Primary industry, including agricultural products, minerals and utilities, remained a significant sector.

Ten years later, in 1991, the picture was dramatically different. The numbers employed in manufacturing had almost halved, while the numbers employed in financial and business services had increased by almost one quarter. By 1998, manufacturing employment was almost half what it had been at the beginning of the 1980s, while financial and business services employment had doubled. After declining between 1981 and 1991, employment in distribution, hotels and catering increased by over one quarter in the 1990s, and primary services shrank to a negligible share of London's workers.

With these dramatic changes it seems little exaggeration to say that the London of 2001 is not the same economy as the London of 1981. Two

Table 1.2 Greater London: employees by sector between 1981 and 1998

	1981		1991		1998		Change 1981–1991		Change 1991–1998	
	000s	*%*	*000s*	*%*	*000s*	*%*	*000s*	*%*	*000s*	*%*
Primary industry	130	4	77	2	13	1	-53	-69	-64	-83
Manufacturing	611	17	323	11	282	8	-289	-89	-41	-13
Construction	161	5	118	4	116	3	-43	-36	-2	-2
Distribution, hotels and catering	687	19	646	20	812	24	-41	-6	166	26
Transport and communications	368	10	308	9	295	8	-61	-20	-13	-4
Financial and business services	566	16	734	23	1,155	32	168	23	421	57
Public admin and defence	193	5	248	8	220	6	55	22	-28	-11
Education, health, other services	841	24	801	25	736	20	-40	-5	-65	-8
Total	*3,558*	*100*	*3,254*	*100*	*3,630*	*100*	*-304*	*-9*	*376*	*12*

Source: Office for National Statistics (ONS)

Note: 1981 and 1991 standard industrial classification (SIC) 1980, 1998 SIC 1992

related developments explain these changes: the decline of the manufacturing industry and the rise of services.

Decline in manufacturing production

The decline in manufacturing in London can be associated with a fall in
the production and market for a range of goods. Prime place should go to
metal products. As a material, metal has been replaced by plastic. At the
same time, all labour-intensive production systems have seen severe
competition from Asia and developing countries, whose wage costs have
been much lower than in Europe and the United States. In the 1990s,
these economic forces included 'globalisation'. Companies have adopted a
global market – producing goods wherever in the world it has proved
cheapest. Globalisation strategies have been encouraged by the liberalisation of global trade regulations, a relative decrease in transport costs and
the achievement of economies of scale by concentrating global production
in a few key plants.

The rise of IT and telecommunications – forces more usually associated with the expansion of the service sector – is also having an increasing
impact on manufacturing. For example, a combination of computer aided
design (CAD), e-mail and computer aided manufacture (CAM) can allow
design facilities on one side of the globe to programme machinery to
mould, cut and otherwise create a new product on the other side of the
world. Such developments are by no means yet exhausted and it is reason-
able to expect the manufacturing environment to become more competitive. Increased competition and automation will continue to put pressure
on manufacturing jobs in London for some time to come.[1]

These developments have, however, led London manufacturing to
become 'lean and mean'. The high property and transport costs characteristic of London and other large cities discourage large labour-intensive factories, but the huge creative talent of London has maintained its
lead in manufacturing design. London's strategic global location, its
financial centre, telecommunications infrastructure and world hub
airports all make it a good place for a company HQ. Transport and

---

[1.] See London Skills Forecasting Unit, *Production Skills in the Digital Economy* (2001).

telecommunications links mean that designers in London can work for manufacturing plants around the world.

Table 1.3 shows how the overall monetary value of manufacturing production in London has increased. The overall value increased from £9,999 in 1988 to £11,381 in 1997. This value has represented a diminishing share of UK production. Nevertheless, when the value of production is seen per employee it can be seen that employees in London produce more per person than the UK average – manufacturing workers in London are more productive. Since 1988, London manufacturing has become increasingly productive, maintaining a 10 per cent advantage over the average for the United Kingdom.

Although employment in London's manufacturing is expected to decline, economists generally believe that the sector has 'stabilised' and will not suffer such a precipitous decline in the future as it did in the 1980s.

Table 1.3 Gross value added in manufacturing[1,2]

	London (£ million)	London as a % of United Kingdom	£ per GVA employee London	United Kingdom
1988	9,999	9.6	22,520	20,597
1989	10,518	9.5	24,787	21,901
1990	9,986	8.7	25,429	23,091
1991	10,379	9.1	27,141	23,514
1992	9,976	8.7	28,801	24,819
1993	9,544	8.2	30,326	27,093
1994	10,643	8.5	34,171	29,378
1995	11,430	8.3	34,765	30,868
1996	11,130	7.9	37,097	33,106
1997	11,381	7.9	37,812	33,614

1 Data for 1987–1992 are based on SIC 1980; data for 1993 onwards are based on SIC 1992.

2 At basic prices.

Source: Annual Business Inquiry, Office for National Statistics

Jobless growth

Developments such as those in manufacturing where automation and IT developments have allowed growth in production with limited growth in employment have been described as 'jobless growth'. Some manufacturing industries and other sectors experienced major production and sales growth in the 1980s and 1990s, but this has not led to a great expansion in employment. New technology has allowed employers to increase productivity – the amount produced per employee. More productive plants can be more efficient, resulting in more competitive, lower priced goods.

'Jobless growth' has affected all industries. Indeed, the term 'jobless growth' is not a particularly useful concept since it is true to say that the major change is that productivity has increased, thus creating a more competitive business environment. An industry characterised by 'jobless growth' would be one that has seen a higher growth in productivity and output with little change in employment levels. In fact, wherever there has been growth in production, some growth in employment has taken place, but a general increase in productivity means that growth produces fewer new jobs than it used to.

Furthermore, London's employment has risen as a share of national employment. In 1991, 14.7 per cent of all the jobs in England were based in London. In 1998, this had risen to 15.1 per cent of English jobs. The proportion of jobs based in northern England fell during this time, and

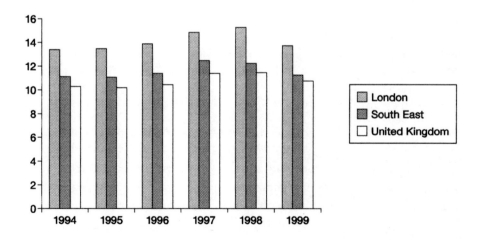

Source: DTI Regional Competitiveness Indicators, March 2001

Figure 1.1 VAT registrations as a percentage of overall stock of registered businesses

only South East England saw a rise in the proportion of English jobs that was greater than that of London.[2]

One aspect of continuing growth in London is new firm formation. When expressed as a percentage of the overall stock of businesses, the number of firms registered for VAT in London was higher than in any other region of the United Kingdom, every year from 1994 to 1999 (Figure 1.1), in both services and manufacturing.[3] Unfortunately, the survival rate of these new businesses is poorer than in most regions of the United Kingdom, with less than 60 per cent of businesses established since 1991 surviving for more than three years. This suggests that Londoners have a high level of entrepreneurship within a turbulent business environment (more on this later). London's growth may therefore be built on the back of failure, as entrepreneurs learn what works and what does not through experience.[4]

Operating in London entails high costs with regard to housing, premises and transport. Businesses that are likely to pay these in return for other advantages are those:

- that almost operate without external services – small businesses with high value added;
- innovative businesses that seek external links to support R&D or finance;
- with few transport dependencies – few staff, producing information goods;
- with international markets;
- based around strategic functions – HQs that need to be close to national government.

In fact, at establishment level there is no evidence that London employers tend to be smaller than in the country as a whole – indeed, in the City they are significantly larger (although single plant firms do appear to be more important in other parts of London). Comparison of the characteristics of over- and under-represented sectors in London, drawing on data from the

---

[2] DTI Regional Competitiveness Indicators, March 2001.
[3] The smallest businesses are not eligible for VAT, although the threshold at which payment starts has varied over time.
[4] Ibid.

1996 London Employer Survey (Gordon and McCann, 1998)[5] supports most of the other hypotheses however. In particular, concentration in London was associated with:

- market areas: mainly outside the South East, particularly in Europe;
- purchasing areas: either mainly in London or else no significant purchases from anywhere (together reflecting an absence of constraint on London locations, rather than a positive location factor);
- market type: selling directly to firms, and not to government;
- product innovation: rated as very important;
- establishment function: not mainly engaged in production or logistics but administration, sales or service provision;
- product cycle: market not strongly declining; and
- external advice: using private consultants/professionals for external advice (rather than only official bodies, or nobody).

Rise of service industries

The major increase in service sector employment can be attributed to many of the same forces which hindered the development of manufacturing employment. Manufacturing companies were finding it hard to compete against lower unit labour costs in the developing world. Service sector companies were finding that they could increase their profits without such competition. The 1980s witnessed the development of world-leading advertising and consultancy firms in London. Their growth was spurred by:

- the expansion of the financial sector in the City, which provided a ready market for their services;
- the outsourcing of company functions such as marketing, purchasing and IT, following management trends to 'delayer' organisations. Consultancies could run these outsourced functions; often by employing those who previously worked for the client company;
- the availability of highly skilled workers, as a result of outsourcing and as a product of first-world educational systems.

---

5. I R Gordon and P McCann, 'Industrial clusters: complexes, agglomerations and/or social networks', paper presented to Regional Science Association, British and Irish Conference, *Urban Studies*, May, 2000.

1990s' developments in IT and telecommunications encouraged this development. IT has allowed information 'products' to be tailored and marketed to particular client groups. Telecommunications have enabled such goods to be distributed around the world with minimal cost. These developments have led to descriptions of the 'information economy' and, during 2000, the 'new economy'.

These developments go some way to explaining the rise in employment in financial and business services between 1981 and 1998, as shown in Table 1.2. The rise in service sector employment also directly affected employment in distribution, hotels and catering by creating a wide range of people who needed to network and exchange information in cafes and hotels. Data[6] indicate that domestic visitors to London rose by around 20 per cent each year between 1994 and 1997, while annual foreign visitors rose by over 10 per cent in 1994 and 1995. These increases indicate the extent to which rising visitors in the 1990s stimulated growth in employment in hotels and catering. Hotels and catering in London would also seem to involve a substantial overseas market (see Table 1.4).

'Information economy'

The growth of service industries has been associated with the development of the 'information economy'. This term reflects the 'commodification' of information. Information is becoming increasingly differentiated as a product which can be traded using telecommunications and the Internet. Financial and insurance policies, for instance, can be tailored and packaged to the needs of particular client groups by age, gender, income etc.

The result of this growth in information products has been the development of 'new sectors' – groups of firms with particular products aimed at particular markets. Manufacturing firms can easily be classified by physical product. Service industries are much more difficult to classify as their products are 'electronic' or 'invisible', and many of their products and sectors are still evolving into clear markets. For example, the revolution in electronic design has led to a convergence of broadcasting, film,

---

[6]   London Research Centre, Government Office for London, Office for National Statistics, *Focus on London 2000*, London (2000).

Internet, telecommunications, publishing and other industries involved in putting together sound and images to transmit them around the world. Out of this mix has emerged the 'New Media' sector – specialist companies that design products on computer using 3D sound and animation, as well as other new 'digital' techniques.

The London Employer Survey has differentiated companies by the functional roles they fulfil in addition to their industrial classification.[7] A sector analysis of the London economy gives only an approximate picture of the actual day-to-day business carried on at many establishments. Figure 1.2 shows the proportion of establishments that carry out service delivery compared to the proportion that are actually engaged in a different form of activity.

The main activities that escape simple sectoral analysis include:

- Headquarter functions related to the management of group activities: these were estimated as the primary function of 4 per cent of London establishments.

Sector	Basic v. other functions		Key 'other functions'
Manufacturing	78%	22%	Delivery of manufacturing services; sales; design
Construction	80%	20%	HQ functions; sales; routine office functions
Retail/ Wholesale	89%	11%	HQ functions; production
Hotels/ Restaurants	90%	10%	HQ functions
Transport and Communications	64%	36%	HQ functions; sales;
Financial Services	85%	15%	HQ functions; sales; routine office functions;
Business Services	75%	25%	HQ functions; sales; design

Source: London Employer Survey 1999.

Figure 1.2 Major business sectors; proportions of establishments by function

---

[7] This section is drawn from primary analysis of the 1999 London Employer Survey carried out by Prism Research Ltd.

- Sales functions: selling is not just the preserve of retail and wholesale outlets. For example, 20 per cent of work places in the communications sector, 9 per cent in financial services, 11 per cent in business services and 4 per cent in construction and manufacturing saw their primary activity as selling. As these establishments were relatively small, their proportion of sectoral employment was low.
- Routine office functions: similarly, routine clerical/data processing activities were also sometimes identified as the main activity.
- Design functions: manufacturing and business services identified design as the major business activity on site in 3 per cent and 6 per cent of cases, respectively. The overall percentage of 2 per cent of establishments identifying design as their principal function perhaps minimises the actual significance of this activity – grossed up, the figure suggests that around 7,500 London work places are principally concerned with design. Design establishments tend to be small, accounting for around 1 per cent of employment.

The concentration of London's industry in a particular range of functions suggests that the capital's industrial structure is not best characterised by the Standard Industrial Classification (SIC) or by functional categories. The functional activities reflect the growing convergence of different industries, exemplified by the importance of sales and design in Figure 1.2. However, the functions that are distinguished in Figure 1.2 do not follow a strict classification of activity. They serve to illustrate that London's economy is not simply characterised by certain sectors, but by certain kinds of activity. For example, sales typifies London as a great metropolis in which business is conducted face to face. Businesses are located in London in order to be able to interact closely with government, global finance and other services. The significant part played by design in Figure 1.2 reflects the creativity of Londoners. London is a rich source of cultural and ideological variety. It is a magnet for creatives who can find both colleagues to develop new ideas and a large audience open to new ideas in technology, expression and entertainment.

Growth, unemployment and the 'new economy'

In the 1990s, the United States witnessed the most prolonged period of growth in its history (Figure 1.3), which led some economists to

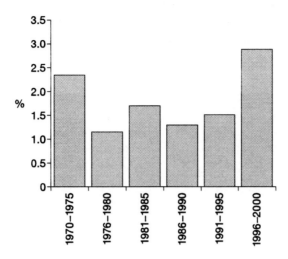

Source: US Department of Labor, *The Economist*

Figure 1.3 Productivity growth in the United States

question whether the 'boom and bust' law of the business cycle still existed.

Economists debated whether they should tear up their textbooks, and coined the term the 'new economy' to describe the conditions that have seemingly broken the rules of economics. The conditions for the 'new economy' may also exist in London. They could lead to continuing growth in output and falling unemployment. However, this growth is fragile and depends on whether companies can improve their current level of innovation and diversify recruitment to employ more people from those areas of London where unemployment is still well above the average for the United Kingdom. During late 2001, events have suggested that a global economic downturn and a return to the business cycle have indeed arrived, but the forces of the 'new economy' are here to stay and it is worth examining them in some detail to see how their longer-term influence may still be felt.

Standard economic theory sees unemployment held to a 'natural' or 'structural' level by the business cycle. The expectation has been that, with the lowest rate of unemployment in London and the United Kingdom for over 20 years, wage inflation would increase as the overall (net) number of workers available for work (ie the unemployed) fell, and prosperous companies would increasingly be competing to attract the most highly skilled workers. Wage inflation leads to rising wage bills and hence to reduced recruitment. Unemployment would then rise and return to its normal 'structural' equilibrium. However, until 2001, the US economy continued to grow despite extremely low levels of unemployment. Some economists have talked of a 'new economy' in which IT developments including the Internet have led to a new, lower level of structural unemployment.

The Bank of England[8] believes that the purchasing power of employees' wages may have been boosted by tax concessions and relative falls in import prices as a result of the high value of sterling. This relative rise in purchasing power reduced demands for pay rises, and maintained a lid on inflation. An OECD report[9] in 2000 concluded that Britain's current unemployment rate was lower than its 'structural' rate because the country was going through a short-term period of adjustment when economic conditions were particularly benign. The implication is that rather than achieving stability at the new low rate of unemployment, economic forces would drive unemployment up again within a few years.

As far as London is concerned, it might be possible to consider a level of 'structural unemployment' in relation to that of South East England. It has been suggested[10] that the unemployment rate in South East England needs to fall below a level of 3 per cent before there is an improvement in unemployment in London relative to that region. These conditions have applied since 1997 but it will take between six and sixteen years of positive economic conditions to bring unemployment rates in the two regions into line. This relationship shows how London's growth in employment is linked to the wide prosperity of South East England.

Another element in the 'new economy' is productivity. The United States' remarkable rise in GDP has been driven by a strong rise in productivity. It is thought that this growth in productivity is driven partly by making better use of 'under-utilised' employees, and partly by IT

---

8   Bank of England Inflation Report, August 2000, pp 30 and 56–7, suggesting that earnings growth in the United Kingdom has been lower than expected and may well continue to be so for the next two years.

9   P Richardson et al, 'The concept, policy use and measurement of structural unemployment: estimating a time varying NAIRU across 21 OECD countries', *OECD Economics Department Working Papers* (2000), 23. They estimate that in the United Kingdom the current unemployment rate and the 'short-run' structural unemployment rate are below the equilibrium or medium-term structural unemployment rate. The time lag for 'short-run' structural unemployment rate is 'dependent on analysis'.

10 Corporation of London, *London–New York Study* (2000), pp 18–19, after work by Nick Buck and Ian Gordon.

developments.[11] Just under half of employers in the 1999 London Employer Survey said that their productivity had improved. Productivity improvements were particularly common in the service sectors and medium-to-large employers. Furthermore, the most common explanations for productivity improvements were 'pushing staff harder' (30 per cent) and new technology (23 per cent).

There are thus suggestions with regard to wage inflation, unemployment and productivity that London is benefiting from a 'new economy' effect. However, productivity (particularly the element derived from IT) will need to be improved, and recruitment diversified, to maintain London's place in the 'new economy', and to continue to reduce the level of unemployment.

London: global city

Table 1.2 suggested that London in 1998 was dependent on a narrower range of industries than it was in 1981. In particular, it has sometimes been suggested that if the City lost its global position in financial services, other service industries would not survive. This picture is misleading however. First, Table 1.4 has shown that much more employment is dependent on the rest of the United Kingdom than on international markets. Second, discussion of the 'information economy' has demonstrated the complex nature of the service industry in which new sectors and new markets are emerging. Many of these services are not solely reliant on either manufacturing or financial services and many have completely independent markets. The move to an 'information economy' or 'new economy' is not a move to a fragile structure of dependent companies, but a strong lattice of interdependent markets for new types of goals.

Gordon[12] has used LSFU survey data to reallocate employment according to the main market area of the companies concerned. According to this analysis, the sectors which create the most jobs from EU and world markets are, first, financial services and, second, hotels and catering together with other services (Table 1.4).

---

[11] There is a strong argument to say that IT's contribution to US productivity has been exaggerated. See Anatole Kaletsky in *The Times*, 22 August 2000, citing Professor R Gordon of North Western University. In the United Kingdom, this argument has also been advanced by Doug McWilliams of CEBR.

[12] London Skills Forecasting Unit, *London – Understanding the Global City* (1999).

Table 1.4 Distribution of employment by main market area[13]

	Local/ borough	Greater London	South East	Rest of UK	European Union	Rest of world
Agriculture, mining etc	1,000	—	—	2,000	—	2,000
Engineering industries	3,000	14,000	10,000	33,000	6,000	7,000
Paper and printing	12,000	23,000	5,000	37,000	2,000	12,000
Other manufacturing	9,000	24,000	12,000	45,000	3,000	10,000
Construction	15,000	42,000	17,000	12,000	—	1,000
Wholesale distribution	52,000	45,000	25,000	48,000	3,000	10,000
Retailing	225,000	38,000	10,000	21,000	2,000	8,000
Hotels and catering	83,000	32,000	5,000	23,000	18,000	19,000
Air transport	—	—	5,000	21,000	3,000	4,000
Other transport	72,000	53,000	9,000	32,000	4,000	12,000
Financial services	50,000	48,000	12,000	115,000	21,000	50,000
Professions	15,000	33,000	16,000	23,000	3,000	6,000
IT, R&D, telecoms	11,000	42,000	6,000	51,000	4,000	4,000
Other business services	94,000	170,000	57,000	152,000	20,000	19,000
Government	98,000	39,000	12,000	65,000	—	—
Education	136,000	29,000	5,000	14,000	4,000	6,000
Health	146,000	66,000	18,000	36,000	—	1,000
Recreation and culture	46,000	26,000	6,000	34,000	7,000	6,000
Other community services	36,000	15,000	3,000	18,000	1,000	1,000
Total	1,104,000	739,000	233,000	786,000	101,000	178,000

Source: London Employer Survey, 1998

Organisational change

Employers had to deal with an enormous amount of structural, organisational and technological change in the 1990s. The ability of employers to keep pace with these changes is essential if London's position as a global city is to be maintained and enhanced. The European Union and UK government recognise the demands that result for employers, and various programmes have been established to assist organisations with the process of adaptation and change.

According to the London Employer Survey in 1998 and 1999, approximately one-quarter and one-third of medium and large employers respectively experienced substantial change every year. This is a key issue, given the strategic importance of these employers to the London economy and the large numbers of staff potentially affected.

---

[13] Establishments representing a further 6 per cent of jobs refused to disclose their main market area.

The 1998 London Employer Survey found that, overall, 13 per cent of employers in the London area experienced substantial organisational/ structural change in the 12 months prior to the survey. This equates to approximately 42,000 companies across London. Table 1.5 looks at the nature of these changes across employer size bands.

Table 1.5 Organisational change (%)

	All	Small	Medium	Large
Merger	2	1	4	10
Takeover/buy-out	3	3	5	4
Other major reorganisation	9	8	17	23
None of the above	85	86	73	63
Don't know	2	2	2	1

Source: 1998 London Employer Survey
Base: All employers (multiple response question)

Financial services witnessed a high level of change in 1998, but this was followed by a more stable period in 1999. The level of organisational change was particularly high in the transport and communications sector in 1998 and 1999 (17 per cent of employers). This may reflect the pace of technological change in this sector.

Figure 1.4 shows that there were some variations across London. South London had the highest proportion of employers reporting organisational change in the 12 months preceding the survey (17 per cent) and West London had the lowest proportion (10 per cent).

Ethnic minority employers

Ethnic minorities and cultural diversity are a vital element in making London one of the world's leading business centres. London is Europe's gateway to the world. Minority communities in London allow companies to engage with markets and businesses throughout the globe. Ethnic minorities make up one-quarter of London's population and one-fifth of its workforce. The white residential population is declining in numbers. Ethnic minorities are already the majority population in the boroughs of Newham and Brent. As a growing, young population, ethnic minorities are the future of London in terms of both its workforce and the growth of new businesses. As a young population the early work experience of ethnic minorities will form the attitudes that will determine London's future economic base.

The role and performance of ethnic minority employers are of interest from two particular perspectives. The first of these is the particular contribution to London's economy made by the distinctive skills, energies and connections of ethnic minority employers. The second is the contribution that ethnic minority employers can make to the employment and human capital of groups facing discrimination in the labour market.

The 1999 London Employer Survey estimates that 17 per cent of private sector employers in London, employing 230,000 people, are owned by ethnic minority employers.

The most significant ethnic minority employers in terms of numbers employed are from four ethnic groups: Indian, 'Other Asian', 'Other' and 'Mixed white/other' (Table 1.5).[14] Comparison with Census data on the ethnic composition of the resident population in 1991 suggests that the 'Other white' and 'Other' groups each generated a disproportionately

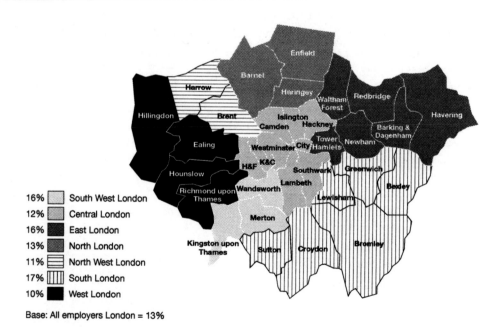

16%	South West London
12%	Central London
16%	East London
13%	North London
11%	North West London
17%	South London
10%	West London

Base: All employers London = 13%

Figure 1.4 Analysis of organisational change

---

14 The ethnic classification used in this report is derived from those used by the Commission for Racial Equality, the 1991 Census, and proposals for the 2001 Census.

large volume of employment compared to their respective shares of the
population, while the share of the 'Other Asian' group was broadly in
line with its population size. Businesses owned by other minorities
were responsible for proportionately lesser amounts of employment,
although the ratio of employment generated to population was much
higher for the Indians and Chinese than for Bangladeshis or Black
groups.

In 1999, the London Employer Survey considered employers of mixed
ownership for the first time.[15] Such mixed employers represented 2.4 per
cent of all private sector employers and employ 2.7 per cent of the London

Table 1.5 London employment of UK-based employers by ethnic origin of owners/directors

Ethnic origin of owners/directors	Estimated employment[16]		1991 Census population
	(000s)	*(%)*	*(%)*
White	1999	84.9	70.1
British	1,770	75.1	71.0
Irish	30	1.3	3.8
Other white	199	8.5	5.3
Asian	*111*	*4.7*	*10.3*
Indian	51	2.2	5.2
Pakistani	6	0.3	1.3
Bangladeshi	1	0	1.3
Chinese	9	0.4	0.8
Mixed white/Asian	8	0.3	-
Other Asian	36	1.5	1.7
Black	*20*	*0.9*	*7.1*
Black Caribbean	6	0.3	4.7
Black African	4	0.2	2.4
Mixed white/black	10	0.4	—
Other			
Other	55	2.3	1.8
Mixed white/other	32	1.4	—
Don't know/refused	125	5.3	—
Total	*2,355*	*100*	*100*

Source: London Employer Survey, 1999
Note: Estimates of Irish and 'Other white' population numbers are based on place of birth data, not ethnicity, with
(white) 'British' as a residual from the Census numbers for white ethnic origin. No estimates for mixed groups are
available from the Census.

---

[15] This could include partnership with directors from different ethnic groups and owners of mixed ethnic
background.
[16] London Employer Survey, 1999.

workforce. When compared with other groups listed in Table 1.5, this means that they represent one of the larger groups of employers, comparable to Asian employers.

Sectoral representation of ethnic minority businesses

The sectoral distribution and the small size of ethnic minority businesses also lend them a particular character. The overall distribution of ethnic minority employers by sector in 1999 corresponded closely with the results of the 1998 survey, with major concentration of ethnic minority employers in wholesale/retail and business services sectors (Table 1.6). The sectoral distribution of ethnic minority employers is compared with that for London as a whole. Ethnic minority employers were more common than one would expect[17] in hospitality and transport/communications (including telecoms). Irish, Black and Indian employers were found less in manufacturing than would be expected from the overall sectoral distribution.

This distribution is similar to that recorded in the Barclays Bank national survey[18] of ethnic minority employers, which recorded 68 per cent of Asian employers in the retail sector.

Market and function of ethnic minority businesses

The 1999 London Employer Survey found that ethnic minority employers were more focused on the very local or borough and had a substantial involvement in sales functions (Figure 1.5). Asian people owned over 10 per cent of all direct sales operations, and 9 per cent of all wholesale operations, almost double their share of wholesale/retail businesses. Asian businesses were concentrated in retail operations but were also involved in a wide range of direct sales activity in other sectors.[19] Black Caribbean people owned 16 per cent of all call centres in the survey. Almost

---

[17]   In other words, they were more of them than one would expect from ethnic minorities' share of the London population.

[18]   The Barclays survey had a sample of 510 companies and is obtainable from their web site www.business-park.barclays.com/reviews/ethnic.htm.

[19]   A large group of Indian business owners were, for example, working as direct sales employers in the transport and communications sector. These could, for example, include sales of mobile phones.

Table 1.6 Sectoral distribution of business within ethnic group

	White British	Irish	Other white	Indian	Pakistani/ Bangladeshi	Other Asian	Black	Total
Agriculture and fishing	0.8	0.8	0.5	0.0	0.0	0.4	0.0	0.6
Manufacture	10.0	3.6	3.7	4.1	14.0	6.5	0.9	8.3
Utilities	0.1	0.0	0.0	0.0	0.0	0.0	0.0	0.1
Construction	8.1	27.8	2.2	0.0	3.0	6.1	14.0	7.3
Wholesale and retail	19.0	14.4	27.3	49.4	36.6	13.8	33.3	21.1
Hospitality	4.4	17.7	9.4	8.5	10.8	15.1	4.9	6.0
Transport	4.2	1.0	6.5	8.5	0.9	12.9	5.9	5.2
Finance	3.4	2.4	5.5	5.2	0.0	5.7	3.7	4.0
Business services	39.9	27.2	32.2	17.3	32.7	27.7	31.0	36.9
Public administration	0.0	0.0	0.0	0.0	0.0	0.0	0.0	0.1
Education	3.0	0.0	3.4	1.6	0.0	3.6	1.3	3.0
Health	1.7	5.2	1.8	3.3	0.0	3.5	0.5	1.9
Other community	5.4	0.0	7.4	2.2	2.0	4.7	4.6	5.4
	100.0	*100.0*	*100.0*	*100.0*	*100.0*	*100.0*	*100.0*	*100.0*

Source: London Employer Survey, 1999

one-quarter of strategic sales sites were owned by 'Other white' groups (largely reflecting foreign-owned companies).

The London Employer Survey indicated that ethnic minority employers were heavily involved in direct sales across a range of sectors, and that as direct 'face-to-face' sales operations they were working within a predominantly local market. This finding accords with research by Focus Central London, which suggested that four out of five ethnic minority

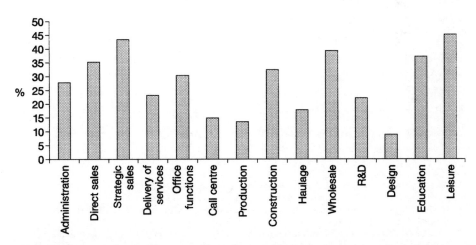

Source: London Employer Survey, 1999

Figure 1.5 Ethnic minority employers by business function

employers sold to individuals rather than to other businesses (including public agencies).[20]

Two different patterns of market orientation were evident. Among Asian and 'Other' groups there was a bi-polar pattern, including an above average proportion serving export markets[21] (perhaps exploiting particular connections), as well as many local employers. Among black employers, on the other hand, the London market assumes much more importance. What the two groups had in common was a relatively weak orientation to the South East and UK markets. However, the predominance of HQ employers over branches in the survey suggests that they should have some branches outside London. Both the localism and the export orientation of ethnic minority employers are associated with particular service activities including distribution, transport and hotels/catering. Hotels figure prominently among employers with an overseas market. Many of the particular market orientations may reflect the difficulties that ethnic minority businesses can face in 'breaking out' from marketing to their own communities.[22]

Commuting and employment

The overall number of people employed in London fell at a broadly constant rate between 1971 and 1996, while employment levels in South East England outside London have risen at a similar rate.[23] During 1988–1996, there was a net loss in South East England of some 10,000 jobs per year.[24] However, in the second half of the 1990s the number of people employed in London began to rise and in 1998 there were over 3.5 million people employed (Table 1.2).

The pattern of job losses in the period from the 1970s to the 1990s reflects the major movement of both individual households and employers from London. Escalating property prices have driven both

[20] *Ethnic Minority Businesses in Lambeth and Southwark*, Focus Central London (1999).
[21] In contrast to 'Other White' strategic sales, these companies were not foreign owned.
[22] *Review of Business Support for Ethnic Minority-owned Businesses in London*, GLE and Middlesex University Business School (2000).
[23] This trend varies according to the business cycle; employment rises (or falls less) in times of prosperity, and falls more steeply than the trend during recessions.
[24] Llewelyn-Davies, UCL Bartlett School of Planning, University of Reading and University of Essex, *The London Study: a socio-economic assessment of London*, Association of London Government (1997).

movements. Households have chosen the cheaper housing and better physical environment outside London. Employers in labour-intensive industries have found it cheaper to attract labour and to obtain new premises with room for expansion outside London. Transport for workers and for goods has also been a major factor.

Data from the London Employer Survey have suggested that despite the overall improvement in employment there may have been a marked increase in companies seeking to move out of London since 1998. Improving global economic conditions and a tightening labour market that has resulted in recruitment difficulties could have occasioned this. Work by Londonomics for the LSFU has suggested that the most important factor in London's competitiveness is the availability of a skilled workforce (see Chapter 3).

Labour participation

In common with the United Kingdom as a whole, the proportion of people who play an active part in the labour force (those in employment and the unemployed) rose markedly in the late 1990s. The overall level of participation among men is lower in London than in the United Kingdom as a whole, reflecting the high level of unemployment and disaffection

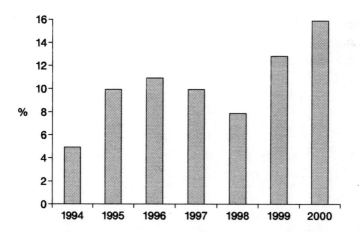

Source: London Employer Survey, 1994–2000

Figure 1.6 Proportion of companies seeking to move in next three years, who would move out of London

from the labour market that is characteristic of urban areas. Nevertheless, recent economic growth has led to men's participation edging closer to that in the United Kingdom.

Women's participation in the labour market has increased more rapidly than that of men. Participation by women has risen more markedly in London than in the United Kingdom as a whole. Women in London often find it more difficult to enter the workforce than in other parts of the United Kingdom. There is a shortfall in the number of childcare places,[25] which also tend to be expensive. Travel is also more expensive than in other parts of the United Kingdom. These high cost barriers for women are often not matched by appreciably higher salaries in London. The barriers are particularly high when women are seeking part-time work. Thus, women in London tend to be more concentrated in full-time, highly paid jobs than elsewhere.

Earnings

This chapter began with a consideration of GDP, the market value of all goods and services produced over one year. Thus, it seems appropriate to

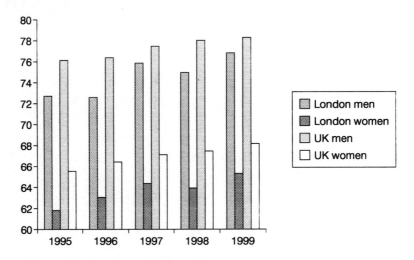

Source: Office for National Statistics

Figure 1.7 Economic activity rates, 1995–1999

---

[25] See *Creating the Learning Capital*, London Skills Forecasting Unit (2001).

finish with an analysis of earnings of Londoners resulting from a higher level of GDP.

Naturally, as a very productive region, with high costs in transport and housing, wages are higher than elsewhere in Great Britain. In 2000, the highest 10 per cent of weekly wages was over £500, over £100 more than for the country as a whole. Even the lowest 10 per cent of employees in London earn considerably more than the lowest 10 per cent in Great Britain as a whole. During the 1990s, the gap between the highest 10 per cent of full-time employees in London and elsewhere in Great Britain rose, but the gap between the lowest earners in London and Great Britain fell (Figure 1.8).

Figure 1.8 shows that those with high incomes in London are increasing their advantage over those in Britain as a whole, whereas those with the lowest incomes in London are losing their margin of extra earnings which helps to pay for higher living costs in the capital. Figure 1.9 demonstrates, as might be expected from the previous paragraphs, that the earnings gap between the richest 10 per cent and the poorest 10 per cent of employees has widened throughout the 1990s, from £400 per week to £650 per week.

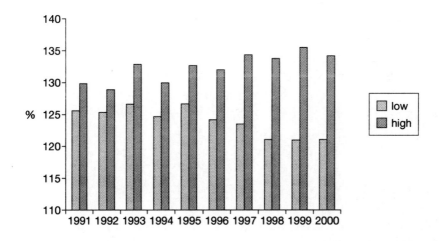

Source: New Earnings Survey, 1991–2000

Figure 1.8 Weekly wages in London as a percentage of those in Great Britain; highest and lowest 10 per cent of employees

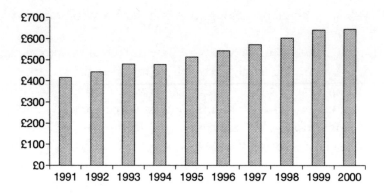

Source: New Earnings Survey, 1991–2000

Figure 1.9 Gap in weekly earnings between top and bottom 10 per cent of employees in London

Conclusion

London has one of the strongest economies in Europe. It leads the world in finance, business services and creative industries. The wide range of ethnic groups present in the City and its world-beating telecommunications and airports make it the leading international gateway of Europe. London's global status is based on its role in financial and business services, but this does not mean that it has a narrow international base. Business services encompass a tremendous range of different services, including emerging new sectors such as New Media.

London's great success means that it is very expensive for both companies and residents. Competition and a finite supply of land raise property prices. High transport and rents must be set against the advantages of being based in a dynamic creative environment, in a capital city with easy access to government and finance. These high costs and the desire for a 'greener' living and working environment have led to an exodus of London residents and companies to other regions, particularly South East England.

The last few years have seen very positive labour market trends, with falling unemployment and rising participation in the labour market. Wages in London have risen faster than in Great Britain as a whole. Unfortunately, the lowest 10 per cent of earners have not shared in this rise in earnings, while many London boroughs are among those with the highest levels of unemployment in the country. Unemployment is the subject of Chapter 6.

2

Economic Geography

Why economic geography?

Geography and economic structures interact in a number of complex ways. For example, the difficulties of transportation across a major city such as London can result in higher costs to business, both in obtaining supplies and distributing their products. The higher costs will make their products dearer and make them more inclined to locate in an area with less congestion and lower costs. Equally, 'creatives' working and living near each other in the West End may find that they benefit from physical proximity through exchanging ideas, learning of new business opportunities, and simply by being in a place that is recognised as a hot bed of new ideas. This tendency for similar businesses to group in a 'cluster' has become central to many government policies, and has in itself led to a revival of interest in economic geography.[1]

This chapter sets out to provide an overview of the economic geography of London. Economics does not follow administrative boundaries and is determined by business benefits such as externalities resulting from the clustering just mentioned. The river is the most obvious geographic feature in London, and yet, since the London docks were wound down in the mid-20th century it has not featured as an economic artery of the city. The river is seldom used for transport of goods and is no barrier to movement of goods to north or south. On the other hand, the boundary of the City – the 'Square Mile' – represents both a physical and economic boundary to the financial district of London, though one which, as we shall see, is quite permeable.

---

[1]   This revival is usually attributed to the work of Michael Porter and Professor Paul Krugman.

London's economic geography may be viewed in a number of ways: one would be to examine the intra-regional disparities purely in labour market terms, covering, for example, skills differentials, training opportunities, wage levels, and so forth. Another approach would be examining Inner London versus Outer London, or East London versus West London, etc. This chapter examines London's economic geography in terms of the distribution of economic activity across, for instance, the City, London Docklands, the Heathrow hub and regeneration areas. This list of the components of London's economic geography is by no means exhaustive – rather, it highlights some of the significant landmarks in the capital's economic geography.

Why is it important to have good knowledge of London's economic geography? Such knowledge sheds light on:

- the underlying currents underpinning change and growth;
- the areas which need monitoring and evaluation for policy purposes;
- the differentials in spatial economic change;
- the policies and actions needed to achieve a more balanced economy.

Geographical perspectives

Economic information for London is available in a number of different perspectives that usually follow administrative boundaries. The smallest unit of geography is the local electoral ward, which builds up to the basic 33-borough structure of London's local government. April 2001 introduced a five-way sub-regional division of London – Central, East, West, North and South – which forms the operational areas of the local Learning and Skills Councils, as well as the delivery arms of business support services offered by Business Link for London.

Such administrative divisions are very convenient for collecting information, but pose a number of problems in interpretation. Economic structures are driven by market forces and rarely respect administrative boundaries. Concentrations of particular industries may lie across the boundary between two or more boroughs. Supply chain links between companies may well be governed more by proximity to a particular major road than location within a particular borough. Large geographic areas may contain particular groups of people or industries that distort the picture of employment. Council estates dominate housing in the City of London and yet the residents present a completely different social profile from the working population that dominates the City in daytime. The residential profile of the Hyde Park area is coloured by particular social groups in that area, as well as by the huge amount of open space, which creates a very low density of housing.

This chapter therefore concentrates on a broad economic picture of London in which the geography is based on economic rather than administrative structures. The uneven economic geography of London manifests itself in a number of ways, and these include:

- Central London's dominance: this area, which covers mainly the City and Westminster, is responsible for approximately 8 per cent of the nation's GDP and nearly 40 per cent of London's output. Around 40 per cent of Greater London employees work in central London. Nearly 90 per cent of central London employees commute in from other parts of London and the rest of the United Kingdom. The City is responsible for generating the vast majority of net overseas earnings, or nearly 85 per cent of the UK total. Central London attracts the majority of tourists to London and is renowned for its 'international' shopping appeal – in Oxford Street and the West End.

- The Inner/Outer London split:[2] Inner London, which is much smaller geographically and has only 40 per cent of London's population, generates 50 per cent of the capital's GDP and has a per capita GDP that is 30 per cent above London's average. Employment in Inner London increased by 15 per cent during 1993–1999, while Outer London assumed a 10 per cent growth. In addition, the average gross weekly earnings in Inner London are 25 per cent higher than Outer, and yet Inner contains most of the areas in the capital with a relatively high 'Index of Deprivation'.

- The East/West split,[3] which shows a broad picture of a relatively more affluent West compared with the poorer East. The West contains the

---

[2] There is no agreed geographical division for London. Our geographical division of London into Inner and Outer is the same as Government Office for London's. Inner London covers the following boroughs: Hackney, Haringey, Islington, Lambeth, Lewisham, Newham, Southwark, Tower Hamlets, Camden, City of London, Hammersmith & Fulham, Kensington and Chelsea, Wandsworth and City of Westminster.

[3] East London covers the following boroughs: Hackney, Haringey, Islington, Lambeth, Lewisham, Newham, Southwark, Tower Hamlets, Barking and Dagenham, Bexley, Enfield, Greenwich, Havering, Redbridge and Waltham Forest.

Heathrow hub (which on its own generates around 5 per cent of London GDP) and a marked concentration of Information and Communication Technology (ICT) firms and other high-tech industries; the East has a larger proportion of derelict (brownfield) land (around 60 per cent of London's total) and contains the largest regeneration project in Europe: the Thames Gateway, extending from east of the City to the Thames Estuary, including south east Essex to the north of the river and Medway towns to the south of the river in Kent. The Docklands (including Canary Wharf) exert an increasing pull on financial firms and hence the City, with the result that new sub-regional administrative boundaries have classified the City as part of the East rather than the Centre.

The following provides an analysis of key aspects of London's economic geography, starting with Central London and then moving to the office market, Heathrow hub and so forth.

The City and financial services

London is one of the three largest international financial centres in the world, alongside New York and Tokyo. London's financial services are geographically concentrated in the City of London. (The City is sometimes referred to as the 'Square Mile'.) In 2000, the financial sector in the United Kingdom generated £32.5 billion worth of net overseas earnings. Approximately 85 per cent of this was earned in the City. This represents a significant contribution to the UK balance of payments, and more so given the serious deficit in the balance of trade in manufactured goods. The financial services sector is a key driver in the London economy, contributing around 31 per cent of London's GDP, and providing 335,500 jobs, or 9 per cent of employment in London in 1999.

Figures (October 2001) from International Financial Services in London (formerly British Invisibles) show that net overseas earnings of the UK financial sector reached a record £31.1 billion in 2001. This is 62.3 per cent higher than the £19.2 billion recorded in 1995, at current prices (Table 2.1).

One of the key drivers to this growth is the volume of activity in foreign exchange markets, which has expanded rapidly over the past decade, with

Table 2.1 Net overseas earnings of UK financial institutions: summary (£ million)

Activity	1995	2001
Banks (*)	3,207	12,377
Securities dealers	1,243	2,191
Commodity traders *	425	246
Futures and options dealers	340	192
Money market brokers	112	246
Insurance institutions	7,243	7,084
Pension funds	1,849	2,504
Unit trusts	696	1,362
Investment trusts	377	395
Fund managers	425	580
Baltic Exchange	291	327
Lloyd's Register of Shipping	57	61
Non-specified institutions **	2,911	3,842
Total	*19,751*	*31,163*

Notes: * Excluding dealings profits, which are classified as capital transactions
** Equal to the sum of 'total other income' and 'income from direct investment'
Source: International Financial Services in London, The 'City' Table (December 2000)

the majority of this activity conducted by banks. A triennial survey coordinated by the Bank for International Settlements (BIS) among 48 central banks, including the Bank of England, has shown that London has been consolidating its position as the world's biggest centre for foreign exchange dealings, with the volume of business in London growing more quickly than most other countries.

Between April 1995 and April 2001, the average daily volume of dealing in London increased from US$464 billion to US$504 billion, during which time it held over 30 per cent of the world market. The amount of business in the United States and Japan is respectively about one-half and one-third of London turnover. The largest European centres are Germany (daily turnover US$88 billion), Switzerland (daily turnover US$71 billion) and France (daily turnover US$48 billion).

Central London, and more specifically the City, benefits a great deal from the advanced telecommunications infrastructure, which it relies on heavily in its operations. This sector has seen a remarkable growth over the period since 1992. Figures for Central London are not available, but nationally this sector (which has a heavy presence in London) grew by a staggering 65 per cent between 1992 and 2000.

Increasing globalisation and use of IT, rather than weakening the importance of place, have maintained the desire to remain in close proximity.
The 'compulsion of proximity' appears to be strong – the recent City
Research Project found that 75 per cent of firms relocating from Central
London have remained within an hour's travel of the centre. The traditional ways of doing business (face-to-face contacts) remain strong, and in
some cases have been made more important by technological advances.

While retail banks in the high street are easily recognisable, there are
several other types in the United Kingdom, usually specialising in particular markets. Many of these are branches of foreign banks. The London
banking sector is a crucial and integral part of the London economy. Its
broad customer base encompasses individuals, companies and public
sector bodies. In June 2000, this sector employed 222,575 – up by 33,000
since September 1996.

The banking sector consists of both UK banks and foreign banks operating in London. Foreign banks, with assets of £1,060 billion (nationally),
are mainly based in London, serving predominantly an overseas clientele;
the majority of their business is conducted in foreign currency and in
wholesale markets.

Investment banks (also known as merchant banks) do not aim to offer
banking services. Most of their income is derived from corporate
customers arising from mergers, acquisitions, flotations, new issues and
other financial advice. They specialise particularly in corporate finance,
derivatives, investment and international trade. The net surplus on the
flows of investment income has shown a distinct cyclical pattern, falling
from a peak of around £4 billion per year between 1986 and 1989, to just
£150 million in 1991, and subsequently recovering to over £10 billion in
1996. This movement in the surplus is broadly reflected in the balances of
each of the three main components of investment income: direct investment, portfolio investment and cross-border lending.

According to BIS, London has a leading world share in the insurance
sector, particularly in marine and aviation markets – in April 2001, the
United Kingdom's share of total world market was 27 per cent and 37 per
cent respectively, far greater than the share of the United States, Japan,
Germany or France. The overseas earnings of insurance have been
boosted by the recovery of Lloyd's. The insurance industry accounts for
approximately 1.2 per cent of UK GDP and provides employment to
around 370,000 people nationally, and 33,000 (or 9 per cent of UK total)

in London. However, the terrorist attacks of 11 September 2001 in the United States are likely to reduce the overseas earnings of the insurance sector, particularly Lloyd's, in 2001 and for some years to come.

Diverse and sophisticated fund management services developed in the United Kingdom during the course of the last century. The total value of identified assets under management (mostly dealt with in London) had reached over £2,600 at the end of 1999 – up from around £2,000 billion in 1996. Institutional UK clients account for the largest portion of funds (65 per cent of the total) followed by overseas institutional clients (26 per cent) and private UK/overseas clients (9 per cent).

The United Kingdom's strong reputation as an international fund management centre is based on a skilled labour force, liberalised operating environment and strong international orientation. Positive advantages for the United Kingdom internationally include London's ranking as the second largest centre after Tokyo by value of international equity.

Finally, significant future market opportunities exist for the UK fund management services as a result of the growth in the management of other countries' non-domestic portfolios, and also from their strong track record in the marketing of products in Continental Europe, Japan and the emerging economies.

Two other local events are likely to strengthen the position of the City.

Change for the Bank of England and financial regulation

The Labour Chancellor, Gordon Brown, made a surprise announcement on 7 May 2001 that monetary policy was to be put in the hands of a Monetary Policy Committee (MPC) at the Bank of England. (In the minds of the financial markets, this is synonymous with the anti-inflationary zeal of the Bundesbank, and could be expected to support the pound.) The markets are now in a better position to assess how the MPC is likely to act. The City/financial markets received the announcement enthusiastically, with the gilts market rallying substantially on the basis that the long-term inflation outlook had been improved.

The Chancellor made another, subsequent, announcement aimed at strengthening the Securities and Investment Board, now the Financial Services Authority (FSA), to regulate financial services. The responsibility of regulating the financial institutions was moved from the Bank of England to the newly created FSA. Well implemented, the initiative should help the City to maintain and improve its position as a global financial centre. The new framework will provide not necessarily tougher, but more intelligent, regulation. The FSA will regulate not according to institution (bank or insurance company), but the nature of the transaction – the crucial distinction will be between a 'retail' financial product sold to customers and a 'wholesale' product sold by one professional (institution) to another (institution).

In addition, international developments – for example, the liberalisation of trade in services and the establishment of the General Agreement of Trade in Services (GATS) at the end of 1994 – have actually consolidated, not weakened, the City's position in terms of global market share. While New York and Tokyo source a larger volume of business from their domestic markets, London frequently has the largest share of many international financial markets. As Table 2.2 shows, such markets include foreign equity trading, where London has 60 per cent of the world total, foreign exchange (36 per cent) and cross-border bank lending (17 per cent). In other words, the United Kingdom (and the City, where around 70 per cent of these activities are performed) remains in a very strong position despite the emergence of new financial markets such as Hong Kong and Singapore. Germany (Frankfurt) remains small compared to London.

These markets' shares each represent a very large volume of business. The United Kingdom continues to hold about one-quarter of the international insurance market, and in other markets its share has remained stable (eg cross-border bank lending has remained at 18 per cent throughout the period 1996–2001). In overall terms, the UK market share is not

Table 2.2 Share of selected international financial markets

Percentage share of world market	UK	US	Japan	France	Germany
Foreign exchange, April 1995	36	16	10	4	5
Cross-border bank lending, 1996	17	8	14	7	7
Foreign equities turnover, 1996	60	35	1	1	2
Financial derivatives, 1996:					
– exchange-trade	16	36	10	10	4
– over-the-counter	27	20	12	10	5

Source: London Stock Exchange, Bank for International Settlements, Bank of England, IFSL

only ahead of New York and Tokyo, but is also far ahead of the amount of business undertaken in France and Germany.

Central London hotels and offices

Central London is the most dynamic economy in London and the United Kingdom. The area referred to as Central London in this book is shown in Figure 2.1. The area is a region approximately 18 kilometres by 10 kilometres, spanning east to west from Greenwich to Notting Hill and north to south from Camden Town to Camberwell, including the City, Westminster and Docklands.

An expanded view of the City and West End shows the new quarters that are regenerating the hitherto run-down districts of the inner city. Midtown stretches from Holborn to Clerkenwell. The new South Bank cultural quarter follows the river from Westminster to Tower Bridge, and the former Docklands areas run eastwards from Tower Bridge. Loft housing, design studios, cultural industries and a strong night-time economy are diversifying the City fringe.

In 1996, nearly 50 per cent of employment in Greater London was concentrated in Central London, which translates into £67.2 billion of output, or 60 per cent and 11 per cent of London's and national GDP

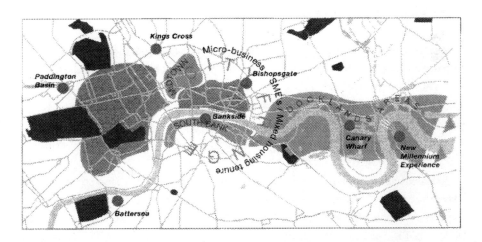

Source: The London Development Partnership, 1998, Preparing for the Mayor and the London Development Agency (first report by the London Development Partnership), p 12

Figure 2.1 Changing central London areas

respectively. The City and Westminster alone account for around 70 per cent of economic activity in Central London.

Over the period 1991–1999, employment in Central London increased by 14 per cent to 1.64 million and contributed over one-third of the total growth in banking, finance, insurance and other business sectors. One-third of employment growth in the distribution, hotels and restaurants sector also occurred in Central London, whereas the public sector experienced a small decline.[4]

The central areas themselves have recently changed significantly and new successful quarters are emerging. These changes include:

- the City fringe immediately surrounding the City and crossing the river into Southwark and Lambeth;
- the new quarter along the South Bank fuelled by burgeoning cultural and creative industries investment;
- the new business quarter at Canary Wharf and the Isle of Dogs, and retail at Surrey docks;
- the Greenwich peninsula with the Dome, the Millennium Exhibition, and the urban village;
- to the east of Canary Wharf, the Royal Docks, also with an urban village, a new university campus, pharmaceutical business investment and – most important in terms of employment – the proposed new Trade Exhibition Centre.

Two other patterns of investment are significant. There is substantial new investment in London hotels, which will do much to support and encourage the visitor and tourism market, a significant business sector in London, and also to open up new areas for tourists. There has also been a substantial opening up of the housing market, particularly in the Docklands area where in the period 1994–2000 almost 20 per cent of London's new housing is being built.

Data obtained from the London Tourist Board show that up to December 1997, 32 new hotels had opened, offering 2,150 rooms. There were also 23 hotels under construction, with 3,960 rooms, to be opened between December 1997 and the end of 1999. In addition, 45 planning consents for hotel development had been given, with potentially 6,980

---

4   Office for National Statistics, 1998.

rooms to be added to the existing stock. A locational analysis of these developments would obviously be useful from a transport planning perspective but this is outside the scope of this report. However, the new developments no doubt reflect a growing demand for tourist-related activities and clearly indicate that tourism itself is a growth sector for the future. In 1999 and 2000, London hotels achieved an occupancy rate of around 80 per cent.

Despite the 1990–1992 recession, demand for offices has been less volatile than supply. Take-up (a measure of demand) in the City and West End peaked in 1987 at around 3.2 million square feet, before reaching a 10-year low of 1.5 million square feet in 1991 and now (2001) it stands at 4.7 million square feet. On the supply side, available office space in the City and West End, taken together, peaked in 1991–1992 at around 20.5 million square feet. This put into perspective the collapse of the office market in the last recession and the steady decline in supply ever since. The office supply stands at around 7.2 million square feet, as at the end of Q2 2001.[5]

The (office supply and demand) situation in Mid Town (WC1-WC2) mirrors the picture in Central London (including the Docklands). Figure

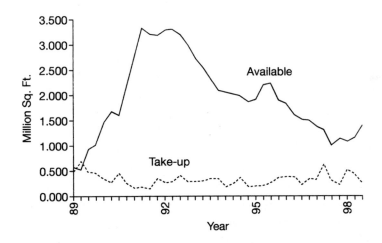

Source: DTZ Debenham Thorpe, 2001

Figure 2.2 Mid-town office market: take-up and available

---

[5]   Insignia/Richard Ellis, Autumn 2001.

2.2 shows how supply is now moving more or less at the same pace as demand.

Vacancy rates in Canary Wharf have fallen to an all-time low, removing a major drag on London office property prices. Figures from FPD Savills (a property agent) show that only 2 per cent of space is now available in the Docklands development following Bank of New York's deal to take on two upper floors at 1 Canada Square. In addition, HSBC is moving all of its City operations into a purpose-built tower adjacent to the existing structure at 1 Canada Square.

One of the main reasons why a number of large firms have moved from the City to the Docklands is the shortage of prime developments with large space for trading purposes. Another reason is the corporate restructuring and re-engineering, implying changing (management) requirements, rather than overall growth in office demand *per se*.

Heathrow hub

The air transport sector in London has developed significantly during the last four decades and substantial investment has taken place. The development of Heathrow during this time has been significant and the airport handled over 61 million passengers (including interlining) in 2000. Gatwick handled 25 million passengers in 2000 compared to 4.6 million in 1971. Stansted handled around 5 million passengers in 2000, an increase of nearly 19 per cent over 1992. The London City Airport handled 250,000 passengers in 2000 and was forecast to handle a total of 450,000 in 2004.

Heathrow is situated in the southern extreme of the London Borough of Hillingdon. Part of the airport extends into Hounslow and Spelthorne in Surrey. It is within easy commuting distance of the London Boroughs of Ealing and Richmond-upon-Thames and the counties of Buckinghamshire, Surrey and Berkshire. Road and rail access to Heathrow is severely congested in part. The main approach from central London is via the A4/M4 and there is direct access from the central area to the national motorway network via the M4 and M25. The A30 links Terminal 4 and the cargo centre to central London and the rest of the road network. The London Underground network has served Heathrow since

1977 and there is also an express rail link to Paddington station on the western fringe of Central London.

Heathrow's World Cargo Centre is the second busiest air cargo port in Europe next to Frankfurt, and it handled over 900,000 tonnes of cargo in 1999, valued at nearly £50 billion worth of goods. This accounts for some 70 per cent of the nation's trade through the United Kingdom's airports.

The airport is owned and operated by the British Airports Authority (BAA plc). Heathrow's passenger capacity with four terminals is around 61 million. In 2000, its passenger throughput stood at 67 million and with the continuing growth in demand for air transport services there is a striking need to meet this demand if London is to maintain its competitiveness. In an attempt to do so, BAA plc has submitted planning proposals for a fifth terminal, adding capacity to cater for a further 30 million passengers per annum (mppa) forecast to materialise by 2016. This will mean increasing the airport's total passenger capacity to 90 mppa.

Several reports have shown the primacy of Heathrow in comparison with other international airports, rendering it a substantial 'operation' which will have an effect on the economy outside the actual perimeters of the airport itself. The *London: World City* report,[6] for example, states that 'London's Heathrow ranked ahead of all other world city airports (Paris, Frankfurt, Berlin, New York and Tokyo) in terms of international passenger throughput'. It currently stands as world leader on international air transport movements and in fourth place by cargo throughput (in tonnes) where Tokyo's Narita Airport ranks first. 'London is now reaping both the negative and positive consequences of being the premier international air services hub in Europe and perhaps the world' (1991, *London: World City*, p 136).

Heathrow has experienced significant growth over the last four decades, successfully responding to growing demand. As noted earlier, in 1994 the airport handled 51 million passengers and 967,000 tonnes of cargo. These goods and people need to be delivered to the airport, they need to be processed and safely handled, and they need to be transported to and from the airport. Table 2.3 shows the scale of the operations and the extent of the airport's growth since 1951. Absolute growth in all three measures was experienced between 1990 and 1992 during a period of national economic decline. While the trend is on the increase, the decline

---

[6] London Planning Advisory Committee, 1991.

Table 2.3 Growth of Heathrow's activity between 1951 and 2000 ('000s)

Year	Terminal passengers	Air transport movements	Total cargo throughput (tonnes)
1951	372	35	10
1994	51,362	409	967
2000	66,980	570	1,134

Note: Figures exclude the helicopter air link movement between the airports of Heathrow and Gatwick
Source: BAA plc, Report and Accounts

in passenger throughput of 2.5 million during the period 1990–1992 can be largely attributed to the Gulf War. This positive trend, however, suggests strongly that the underlying growth potential for Heathrow is considerable and, as noted, its contribution in such times will have added significantly to London's economy.

Heathrow is the world's busiest international airport in terms of international passengers (see Table 2.4), and the largest airport in the United Kingdom over the last 20 years, with nearly 41 million passengers in 1993, more than twice those of Gatwick, the second largest airport in the United Kingdom. The same applies to both air transport movements (number of flights) and cargo throughput.

As a facilitator, Heathrow is important to so many businesses in London and the rest of the United Kingdom. The London Chamber of Commerce and Industry's business survey conducted in 1995 showed that the airport offers locational advantages stemming from business agglomeration in one geographical location, for example externalities in terms of availability of adequate labour, thus reducing costs. In this sense, the survey confirmed

Table 2.4 Ranking of airports worldwide for number of international passengers handled, 2000

	World ranking	Passengers (million)
London Heathrow	1	40.84
Frankfurt	2	25.20
Hong Kong	3	24.42
Paris CDG	4	22.33
Amsterdam	5	20.66
New York Kennedy	9	15.01
Bangkok	10	12.76

Source: BAA plc, CAA, AACI

conclusions of earlier studies examining the importance of Heathrow to industry in the area, in particular along the M4 corridor.

Heathrow has also been able to attract and hold some of the most important players in the industry; this is clearly visible from the extensive list of airline operators (over 90 in 2000) and destinations offered in 2000 (135, compared to 102 for Paris Charles de Gaulle, 73 for New York, 32 for Tokyo and 98 for Frankfurt).

Direct on-airport employment grew from 30,081 in 1961 to 52,272 in 1991, and to 61,240 in 2000 – in other words, employment more than doubled over 40 years. This is naturally due to growth in passenger and cargo throughput. Employment at Heathrow constitutes a significant proportion of total employment in the immediate vicinity. In 1998, nearly 50 per cent of people directly employed at Heathrow came from Hounslow, Hillingdon, Spelthorne, Harrow and Ealing.

However, it should be emphasised that total employment impacts of Heathrow include not only the direct on-airport employment, but also the indirect off-airport employment, indirect employment and induced employment. It is estimated that the current total employment impact of Heathrow is approximately 110,500 jobs.

Figures of overseas visitors to London and the United Kingdom using Heathrow and Gatwick show that 58.8 per cent of all London's overseas visitors depart from Heathrow. In other words, Heathrow handled 5.4 and 2.0 million visitors to Greater London and the rest of the United Kingdom respectively in 2000, and whose expenditure was £2.7 billion and £1.2 billion in London and the rest of the United Kingdom respectively – that is, 21.3 per cent of total UK overseas visitors and 18.5 per cent of expenditure.[7]

To gain a qualitative view of the benefits of Heathrow to businesses in its hinterlands, the LCCI conducted a business survey of firms located around Heathrow during the first two weeks of November 1993. While the data are old, they still provide an indication of the (economic) linkages with the surrounding business community. The survey covered two distinct geographical areas: Inner and Outer. The Inner area is drawn closely around the airport, while the Outer area covers most of the rest of London and parts of Slough and Windsor.[8]

---

[7] These figures were derived using research undertaken by the London Tourist Board and Convention Bureau, October 2001.

[8] A random sample of 4,000 firms was chosen. 927 companies returned completed questionnaires, giving a response rate of 23 per cent. The results were weighted to make the results representative of the industry and size structure of companies in both survey areas (1995).

The following provides a flavour of the results:

- Almost 85 per cent of respondents in the Outer area and almost 80 per cent of companies in the Inner area used air travel.
- Approximately 80 per cent of respondents in both areas used Heathrow.
- There were approximately twice the number of companies using passenger travel than there were using airfreight.
- Almost all companies that required their staff to travel by air used Heathrow. Gatwick appeared less popular, cited by 80 per cent of respondent companies in the Outer area who required their staff to travel by air and 60 per cent of similar companies in the Inner area.
- The majority of companies that used airfreight used Heathrow. Gatwick was used by only 40 per cent of companies that moved goods by air and very few of them used any other airport.

In summary, the airport is linked strongly to its hinterlands. Heathrow is located in an area with stronger economic performance and dynamism compared to London and the United Kingdom in terms of output, personal income and consumer spending. Heathrow is evidently a strong catalyst in this performance. As a facilitator of activity in the tourism and the financial and business services sectors, Heathrow is making a significant contribution to local, London and national economies.

Business surveys show that Heathrow takes a sizeable share of the amount of air travel undertaken by firms in its immediate hinterlands and beyond. In the long term, air transport for both leisure and business is expected to increase. Although the terrorist attacks in the United States have proved a considerable setback for both airlines and airports (particularly Heathrow with its strong transatlantic links), it can be expected that growth of freight and passengers will return, perhaps as early as 2002.

The business survey results also highlight a number of caveats, namely congestion difficulties and competition from both the Channel Tunnel and Gatwick. Congestion puts limitations upon their companies' activities, particularly in the Inner area. An expansion of Heathrow without an improvement in the local road network could possibly limit the benefits of the road network to existing users, and deter potential users. In addition, there is the expectation that the Channel Tunnel may take some business away from Heathrow.

Finally, employment impacts also translate into contributions to the National Exchequer by generating various types of taxes, including a direct airport tax and income tax, which has been quantified in this report. Heathrow contributes at least £0.4 billion to finance government expenditure across the United Kingdom. Heathrow thus provides substantial economic benefit for much of the country, in addition to being a vital contribution to London.

London's regeneration areas

Adjacent to the growth poles of West and Central London are areas of exceptionally high unemployment and social deprivation. It is commonly claimed that there are enough job opportunities in London for all the unemployed that live there. In practice, however, the potential for people who live in these areas to obtain jobs is much reduced by lack of skills, social background, ethnicity, transport costs, availability of cheap childcare, and other factors. These areas are also associated with a crumbling physical fabric including derelict buildings and poor services. The areas thus need 'regenerating' by both rebuilding facilities and creating new employment opportunities.

The official name for these is 'regeneration neighbourhoods'. They are important features of London's economic geography in a number of respects:

- they provide material evidence that London is a city of contrasts, a divided city that combines wealth and prosperity on the one hand and poverty on the other;
- any serious long-term analysis of how London works needs to account for the processes underpinning this dichotomy;
- they assist in identifying areas where policy intervention is needed to alleviate the standard of living of deprived local communities so that they can participate positively in fostering London's competitiveness; and
- they provide an opportunity to examine how local participation and capacity building would lessen uneven development across London in the long run.

Figure 2.3 shows key deprivation areas in London. It is clear that, broadly speaking, the eastern side of the capital suffers relatively higher deprivation levels than the west. There are historical reasons for this phenomenon; many parts of London have not shared economic growth in London. The current situation is one of enormous disparities of wealth creation and equality of opportunity, or of wealth and poverty. Alongside economic growth in the City, deprivation is concentrated in Inner and East London down the Lee Valley, to the east on both sides of the river along the Thames Gateway.

London has some of the most deprived areas in the country. London has 68 wards that fall in the top 15 per cent most deprived wards in England (Figure 2.3). All these areas score high on the DETR's 2000 index of multiple deprivation and are characterised by high levels of unemployment, low incomes, unsatisfactory/overcrowded housing, poor/neglected

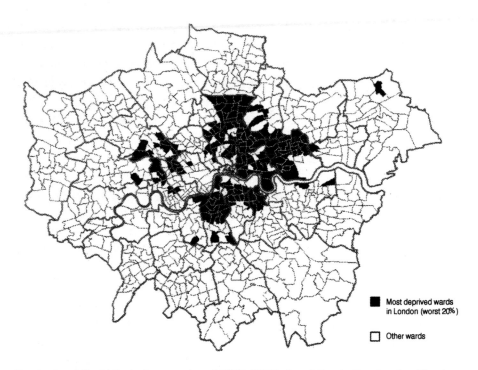

■ Most deprived wards in London (worst 20%)

□ Other wards

Source: Local Social Exclusion mapping of DETR 1998 Index of Deprivation, London Planning Advisory Committee, London Development Partnership, 1999.

Figure 2.3 Disadvantaged communities

environments and high incidence of ill health. Allied with low levels of educational achievement and skills, a substantial majority of people living in these areas have not been able to compete for the new jobs created in London and, consequently, have not been able to share the benefits of economic growth – in short, they have been excluded from economic development in its widest sense.

Consequently, London remains dependent to a very high degree on in-commuters to meet demand for labour in the growing sectors, compounding the consequences of deprivation.

'The core "necklace" of potential rail connections extends from Willesden Junction to Clapham, to Bermondsey, Stratford and Dalston, and back through Camden to West Hampstead, many of the links in this new orbital inner rail loop already exist. In its March 2000 *Building London's Economy*, the London Development Partnership believed that "much could be achieved with relatively modest improvements to exploit the orbital network around the central area and provide better rail access to development sites from areas of high employment". The West London line is one example, where the new interchange at White City will realise substantial regeneration benefits. The East London line extension, which provides access to the area north east of the City, and similarly to the south east, is another example.'

The key demand-side drivers are economic growth and population. The spatial effects of 1990s' growth have been highly focused in certain areas of London: around 65 per cent of total employment growth was concentrated in the City, City of Westminster, Kensington and Chelsea, Hammersmith and Fulham, and Barnet – in other words, growth is concentrated in Inner West/North West London. On the other hand, five boroughs (Waltham Forest, Hackney, Newham, Tower Hamlets and Lewisham) in East London and two boroughs in the south (Lambeth and Croydon) taken together have lost employment during 1991–1998 by 6.3 per cent.[9]

Most of the population growth during 1991–1998 occurred in the west of the capital; around 70 per cent population growth occurred mainly in the boroughs of Barnet, Kensington and Chelsea, Hammersmith and Fulham, Richmond upon Thames and Ealing. The pattern of employment change reveals that while there is still some substance to the historic

---

[9]   Greater London Authority, *Towards the London Plan* (2001).

distinction between East and West London, there was a marked band of low and negative growth running north/south along the Lee and Wandle Valleys.

Trend-based ONS population projections, which reflect historic change, indicate that 63 per cent of population growth (up to 2021) could be expected in Central London and in those boroughs lying to the west. The Greater London Authority (GLA) 'anticipates' the distribution of new housing towards the east, so providing the incentive to shift employment and population to the east alongside the Thames Gateway. The London Plan's distribution of larger housing sites emphasises this point, aiming to alter the historical pattern of economic growth and population distribution.

Inner East London and the Thames Gateway

Another change taking place which is likely to have a significant impact on the future economic geography of London, and London works, is the level of current (and anticipated) economic activity in Inner East London (including the Docklands) and the Thames Gateway area. The demands on London's infrastructure and population created by the challenges of a growing and increasingly globalised economy cannot be met solely through maximising existing locations for economic growth, nor can the projected increase in population be accommodated only in traditional suburban-style residential areas. Pressures on the cost of office accommodation in Central London and on housing in many areas of West and North London mean that London must look beyond established areas to accommodate new growth. The London Plan will set a strategic development focus on East London.

Brownfield sites,[10] mostly located in the Thames Gateway and on the edge of Central London, will be the main focus for development in London. Brownfield land has often been difficult to redevelop because of contamination, fragmented ownership, poor servicing and transport links, and a neglected environment. Priority for the redevelopment of brownfield land will take account of transport accessibility. Where transport accessibility is poor, any case for additional investment in transport must

---

[10] 'Brownfield' sites have already been subject to development some time in the past, as opposed to 'greenfield' sites, which are first-time building on new sites.

take account of development potential. Much of the capacity for development during the course of the London Plan, particularly for housing, will be provided by 'windfall' sites, which are those sites that have not yet been identified by the planning process. The policies in the London Plan will allow these sites to be considered for development in a systematic way.

Canary Wharf's recent success demonstrates that with the right level of commitment and investment, particularly in the transport infrastructure, it is possible to provide quality business accommodation in London that supports and enhances the attractions of the City of London. While it provides a high-quality alternative to the spiralling costs of West End and City office space, its success is that its growth has not been at the expense of growth in Central London – rather it has supported and enhanced such growth. Docklands and the Thames Gateway are the obvious areas where London can realistically provide the additional capacity for the large-volume development needed to attract global institutions to London and retain them. Stratford, due to become a major international transport interchange with the development of the Channel Tunnel Rail Link, can be seen as a key focus for attracting investment and development in a location that is also highly accessible to areas of high unemployment.

Vital to the success of any economic growth in East London will be the opportunity presented to residents of those areas, people who are among the most deprived in the country, to share the benefits of that investment by taking advantage of new jobs. Skill development will be essential and this will mainly be carried out through the interventions of the LDA, Learning and Skills Councils and boroughs. There is also a need to ensure that new development results in community benefits to local people, including design and landscaping, transport improvements and affordable housing.

The Thames Gateway will not only provide much of the capacity for the strategic employment sites, but will also provide a large part of the essential capacity for housing development. Although the boroughs in the Thames Gateway contain just over one-fifth of London's total housing capacity, they include 32 per cent of that which has already been identified; 63 per cent of identified capacity from very large sites (over 500 dwellings) lies within the Thames Gateway. These sites offer particular scope for 'urban village'-type development but many require vigorous joined-up action with the LDA and other partners to bring them forward for development.

The Docklands

The uniqueness of the Docklands experience over the past 20 years merits its own separate section. Within Central London, the City, Westminster and the Docklands account for approximately 75 per cent of employment. While the contribution of the City/Westminster fluctuated around 71 per cent since 1984, the contribution of the Docklands has doubled in the last 12 years, albeit from a small base. In 1984, the Docklands area provided central London with 2.6 per cent of employment, and by 1996 this had almost doubled to 5 per cent. Still, these figures demonstrate the growing significance of the Docklands to Central London (as defined in this chapter), but closer examination highlights the area's growing importance in employment terms to East Central London. Docklands area employment contributed 6 per cent of the East Central London employment in 1984. By 1996, this figure had doubled to 12 per cent. Indeed, it seems as though the Docklands area is increasingly becoming a focal point of employment in East London.

As with London as a whole, the Docklands has prospered due to an ever-expanding base of service sector employment. In 1984, employment in the Docklands was 44,289, with 67 per cent of this in the services sector. By 1996, employment had risen by 86 per cent to 83,701, with 85 per cent of employment in the service sector. Unlike the rest of Central London, official figures suggest that the Docklands area did not experience the massive decline in employment levels in the early 1990s' recession. Rather, the figures suggest that employment has been steadily moving upward (Figure 2.4).

As is well documented, the key growth industries in the Docklands revolve around the financial and business services sectors. Employment in financial intermediation rose from 11,533 in 1991 to 15,481 in 1996. The figures also suggest strong growth in the business services sector, although it appears to have peaked in 1995. With this growing core of global financial players, other support sectors have also benefited. These include growth in sectors such as hotels, restaurants and wholesale retail and repairs. These sectors provide local services to the local financial and business services sector and would perhaps find it difficult to compete if growth in employment in the sector were to slow or evaporate altogether. The recent announcement of the flotation of Canary Wharf and the interest generated as a result, is an indication of increased confidence in the future prospects of the area as a whole.

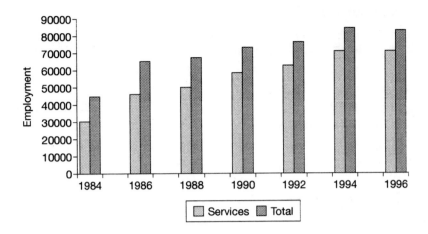

Source: NOMIS

Figure 2.4 Employment in the Docklands

If the remaining infrastructure projects, such as the Jubilee Line extension and the new Exhibition Centre are successful, the area might well overshoot the vision of 175,000 employees in 2014, which was outlined by the Docklands Development Corporation. If, however, the above benefits do not fully materialise, the Docklands area is unlikely to achieve this employment target. New development might shift to West London, particularly the King's Cross or Paddington Basin areas, where there is scope for further development without the need for considerable new (rail) transport capacity.

Broad functional distinctions

To complete this overall picture of London's sub-regional economies, we can add a few observations about the kind of activity that takes place in different parts of London.[11]

As has been demonstrated, West London is the prime gateway to the capital, based around Heathrow and motorway links. Other strengths include high-tech establishments and media. The Park Royal area has a concentration of high unemployment and traditional manufacturing, and is the subject of many regeneration initiatives.

---

[11] These distinctions are based on London TEC Council, *An Economic Profile of London* (1996).

East London was the traditional gateway to London and the major residential area for much of the lower-skilled jobs in the capital. Regeneration, particularly in the Docklands, is transforming this image into that of a new growth pole, but there remain large areas with very high unemployment.

Central London is dominated by the financial district of the City and the major commercial axes of Westminster. The major monuments in and around this area make it the most important generator of tourist income, through hotels and retail outlets. However, surrounding this area are areas of high unemployment, with few economic links to the centres of great prosperity.

The northern and southern London suburbs are the traditional residential areas for the higher-skilled residents of the capital. However, they are also the locations for significant clusters of particular industries. North London has areas of major deprivation and traditional manufacturing similar to those of East London. Textile working is one speciality which has suffered at the end of the 1990s. North London also contains several concentrations of ICT-based media, or New Media, companies.

South London has a major pole of office and HQ development in Croydon, with strengths in many service sector industries. The presence of many rich residential suburbs again tends to distract attention from some areas of higher unemployment.

Table 2.5 illustrates how these sub-regional differences can be seen at borough level. At the bottom of the Table are some of the most 'deprived' boroughs in England, with up to 5 times the unemployment of the more successful parts of London, and only just over half of their population active in the labour market. At the top of the Table is the City, with its tiny residential population and huge number of employed, while the 'dormitory' Borough of Sutton has the highest proportion of economically active, and a tiny number of jobs compared with its residential population.

Table 2.5 shows, in a nutshell, the range of economic and labour market conditions to be found in different parts of London.

ICT and interregional developments

The emphasis in this chapter has been on sub-regional geographies within London; however, it is also important to realise that such economic networks do not respect the boundary of London itself.

Table 2.5 London boroughs: some economic comparisons

	Location	Population in 1998	Employment in 1998 at work places in borough	Unemployment in June 2001, claimants as percentage of employees	Economic activity in 1999, as percentage of residents in labour market	Deprivation rank in 2000, average rank of wards where 1 is most deprived
Some of the most prosperous boroughs						
City of London	Centre/East	5,200	286,500	0	—	205
Westminster	Centre/West	220,800	534,700	0.8	62.7	141
Hillingdon	West	251,200	169,500	1.4	78.8	201
Kingston	South/West	147,300	67,300	1.5	75.7	318
Richmond	South/West	186,700	62,700	2.0	74.3	341
Sutton	South	177,000	56,100	2.3	82.6	254
Some boroughs most in need of regeneration						
Southwark	Centre/South	232,000	133,800	5.3	62.7	9
Islington	Centre/North	179,000	134,300	4.3	63.2	8
Haringey	North	221,600	54,800	10.4	60.7	37
Newham	East	231,300	57,100	10.0	55.8	3
Hackney	Centre/East	194,700	77,100	8.2	56.2	2
Tower Hamlets	Centre/East	181,300	122,800	5.5	51.3	1

Source: Office for National Statistics, 1998–2001

Heathrow has had a major impact to the west of the airport as well as to the east. Its close relationship with the M4 has been an important factor in the development of the high-tech corridor along this route with important nodes at Slough, Reading and Swindon. Equally, to the east of London the rapid growth of a modern office infrastructure in the Docklands has included ICT and Internet hubs. There is now considerable discussion about an East London high-tech corridor to link the Docklands with the science parks of Cambridge.

ICT has found conducive environments within central London, such as New Media in Clerkenwell and broadcasting in Westminster. These are, however, clusters that have been driven by pre-existing strengths in creative industries and telecommunications respectively. Many high-tech firms require new buildings with purpose-built, up-to-date cabling and equipment, with nearby links to satellite and other broadcast stations. As a large city, most of the properties available in London do not easily lend themselves to adaptation to these needs, and thus high-tech companies seek new premises in the M4 and Docklands/Cambridge corridors.

London and the rest of the United Kingdom

The Centre for Economics and Business Research (CEBR) estimates that in 1999 London generated a surplus of almost £13 billion in its trade with the rest of the United Kingdom. Almost £89 billion of London's £127 billion of imports were from elsewhere in the United Kingdom. The CEBR also estimates, therefore, that London's economy supports 4.7 million jobs in the rest of the United Kingdom.

Conclusions

This chapter has concentrated on setting out how the economy of London relates to its sub-regional geography. It has outlined the impact of the major growth poles around the City and Heathrow. It has also set out the degree to which these growth poles sit alongside some of the most deprived areas in the United Kingdom. Finally, the example of the Docklands has shown how one major regeneration area in East London has become a new growth pole.

A number of themes emerge from the analysis in this chapter. This chapter has shown how the economic geography has evolved and is likely to shape in the foreseeable future. It has been argued that the synergy (or otherwise) among these elements of London's economic geography provides clues as to how London works.

The analysis in this chapter suggests that there is a multitude of forces acting upon the economic geography of London – an undercurrent underpinning these changes, which sometimes is not immediately apparent. These forces are shaping different parts (and economic sectors) of London in different ways. Employment in manufacturing has been in decline in all areas of Central London, but the varying forces acting on the capital appear to be channelling employment into the service sectors. For example:

- There has been increasing globalisation and a shift towards the knowledge-based economy, changing sectoral composition and the very nature of individual sectors, with increasing knowledge content in the products and services offered.
- There has been a shifting of the centre of gravity gradually from the west of the capital to the east, ushered by the phenomenal growth in

the Docklands and further away towards the east and the Thames Estuary.

- There have been shifts in the nature of work patterns and skills required to remain engaged in gainful employment, with increasing emphasis on multi-tasking, multi-skilling and flexibility in relations between employers and employees. While this may also be true in other parts of the country, these changes are particularly sharp in London due to its dynamic and sophisticated economy.

In the case of the Docklands, two scenarios appear to be emerging:

- The first is one where key infrastructure projects, referred to above, would materialise. In this case, office development will continue to take place in the east and employment in the Docklands will perhaps exceed 180,000 in 2014.
- The second is one where the full capacity of the new infrastructure (eg the Jubilee Line extension) would be reached in the medium term and, with no additional capacity put in place, office development is likely to move to the west side of Central London. Under this scenario, the Docklands will reach a threshold beyond which it would be more or less impossible to create more office space. Arguably, this would not necessarily be a reflection of lack of demand, but would instead be due to a strained transport infrastructure (including the Jubilee Line extension) which will have reached its maximum capacity perhaps by 2005–2007, if not sooner.

If the second scenario is realised, new office development is likely to locate in other areas west of the City where there is potential for office development – for example, Paddington Basin (around 6 million square feet) and at King's Cross (around 4 million square feet), both of which are well served in transport terms.

3

International Competitiveness

Introduction

London's pole position as an international financial centre is well established. As Chapter 2 demonstrated, London is one of the three largest international financial centres, having a dominant position in certain financial services. However, there is more to a world city and its competitiveness than just the financial sector, as will become clear in this chapter.

The central objective of this chapter is to highlight the undercurrents of London's competitiveness relative to other world cities. It must be emphasised at the outset that the choice of the world cities with which London is compared here has been determined by the paucity of data for inter-city comparison, a fact well known to those initiated in this subject. The comparative variables chosen are also determined by the dearth of data. The discussion has therefore relied on available quantitative and qualitative comparative data, which helps to build a reasonably robust and informative picture about London's competitiveness in comparison with its competitive cities.

This chapter will concentrate on Paris and New York. These cities are most comparable to London as locations of company HQs, world financial exchange and major airports. They compete with London in some of the most significant markets and present the most comparative data.

A world city is a city in which one or more of its economic functions, industries or services is engaged in a global rather than the national (or sub-national) markets. In Chapter 2, the idea of 'globalisation' was briefly discussed. Many cities may be home to some companies that aim to reach global rather than national markets, but there are a few cities which are so dominant in particular sectors that the city economies can be said to be dependent on global as much as on national economic trends. Thus, in the case of London, as was presented in Chapter 1, it has been suggested that the 'meltdown' of global financial markets would lead to economic collapse in London since the capital is dependent on its financial 'heart', the City. It was argued in Chapter 1 and it will be argued again in this chapter that London's competitiveness depends on a wider economic base than financial and business services.

Defining urban competitiveness

A huge amount of literature exists on this subject. The discussion of competitiveness in this chapter is by necessity selective and brief, focusing on key contributions to the debate. In practice, different concepts have been advanced depending on the focus of interest, firm, sector, activity or geographical level.

For a firm, perhaps the most advanced framework of competitiveness is that of Porter.[1] In addition to chance and role of government, Porter's emphasis is on the national/regional influences on individual firms to compete in specific industries in various contested markets. Four sets of conditions form the diamond of competitive advantage, as shown in Figure 3.1.

- Factor conditions, such as skilled labour or infrastructure, which are necessary to compete in a given industry.
- Demand conditions. The nature of home demand for the industry's product or service.
- Related and supporting industries. The presence or absence of suppliers and related industries that are internationally competitive.
- Firm strategy, structure and rivalry. The conditions governing how companies are created, organised and managed, and the nature of domestic rivalry.

---

[1] M Porter, *The Competitive Advantage of Nations* (1990).

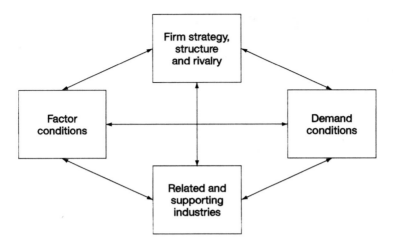

Figure 3.1 Diamond of competitive advantage (M Porter, 1990)

Recent work by Londonomics Ltd for the London Skills Forecasting Unit (LSFU)[2] has reviewed various definitions of business and territorial competitiveness. The review covered definitions advanced by the Eurostat, the London Development Partnership's Competitiveness Group, and the DTI's Regional Competitiveness Indicators. It was pointed out that there was a degree of arbitrariness embedded in sub-national definitions – none clearly relates to a recognised theoretical model (eg competitive or comparative advantage). At an aggregate regional (indeed national) level, sectoral competitive advantage may still be evident and relevant (eg in terms of national market share in a particular global or European market), but there is no simple and satisfactory way of expressing the overall level of competitive advantage possessed by a region. It would thus be quite misleading, for example, to use the overall level of international exports per head (or its share in output) as a measure of competitive success, without regard to the degree to which an area specialised in more/less tradable types of product (eg in manufacturing). In particular, at a sub-national scale, it is quite possible that the quality of non-traded goods/services produced in one area makes an important (positive or negative) contribution to the competitive advantage of traded goods/services produced in other areas.

2   *Global Cities Benchmarking: A Feasibility Study on Performance Indicators and Competitiveness Index for London*, a report submitted to the LSFU, Londonomics, May 2000.

To take London as a case in point, it has been argued that while the concept of comparative advantage tends to focus on costs of factors (mainly labour and capital), other (London-specific) factors need to be taken into account in determining productivity and competitive advantage of businesses (eg in the financial sector). These include, for example: perceptions; quality of life factors; importance of English language; education and training; quality of transport infrastructure etc.[3] These factors are part of London's urban fabric, giving it the capacity to accommodate competitive firms and comparative advantage over other global financial centres, for example.[4]

From this perspective, it can be argued that cities compete by providing a conducive environment for people to live/work in and for local firms to operate efficiently in, thus making particular goods more profitably than others and assuming a larger market share. They compete by fostering the competitive advantage of their firms and also offering a basket of comparative advantage which other cities cannot meet.

The Londonomics report for LSFU was based not only on a literature review, but also on two surveys.[5] On the basis of analysis in the report, Londonomics Ltd advanced the following *operational definition of urban competitiveness* for London:

> *The capacity, under market conditions, to produce goods and services which meet the test of the local, national and international markets, and simultaneously raising the real incomes and quality of life of those who live/work in London, over the long term.*

In other words, London's competitiveness is defined in terms of the capacity of its businesses to meet customer needs in various contested

---

[3] The London Chamber of Commerce benchmarked London against a number of European world cities and certain factors were seen as important for competitiveness, including clean air, quality of health and educational services, quality of public transport, clean streets, lower business costs and providing a skilled labour force (*Evening Standard*, 7 March 2000).

[4] A Hirmis, *London's Competitive Capacity in Europe Post-1992*, Proceedings of Planning, Transport and the Regions Conference, 1992.

[5] The first survey covered eight face-to-face interviews with key people who could provide their perceptions of what constituted urban competitiveness and the factors by which it might be measured. In addition, the team had discussions with heads of research in chambers of commerce, planning authorities and research institutions in 11 'world' cities, exploring the possibilities of obtaining comparable, up-to-date, quality information. A set of quantitative and qualitative indicators had been presented to them, embracing elements of competitive and comparative advantages, as a basis for discussion. They were also asked about their own views of an operational definition of urban competitiveness, which they use for their own cities. The second survey covered 50 London-based companies (see p 12, paragraph 3). It must be stressed that although the surveys covered a small sample of experts, the results nevertheless provide a useful indication of the notions of urban competitiveness and of the indicators that were suggested to measure it.

markets as well as its capacity to meet the economic, social and physical needs of its population and workers. The first half of the definition is more or less a necessary condition for the second, which adds the requirement of the productive use of all the city's assets (full employment) and appropriate investment to secure long-term sustainability.

London's competitiveness is viewed in terms that embrace a host of direct/indirect economic, social and environmental factors (Figure 3.2). For businesses, price remains an important source of competitiveness, but other factors such as quality, customer care and delivery are now also seen as key factors.[6] In addition, a number of respondents to the survey highlighted the importance of political stability and government support for local businesses and the city as a whole.

We believe that this view of London's competitiveness is much fuller than viewing it simply in terms of GDP per head or productivity levels. The Londonomics report suggested that the city's competitiveness could be meaningfully measured using 24 quantitative and qualitative indicators, each of which has varying influence of city competitiveness.[7]

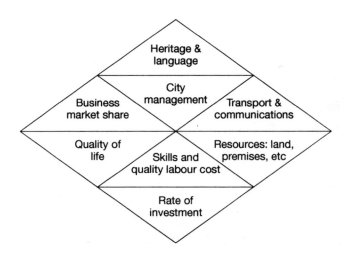

Figure 3.2 Diamond of city competitiveness

---

6   See, for example, summary in LSFU, *Second Annual Report* (2000).
7   The indicators are shown in Table 3.3.

Cities with which London competes

In examining London competitor (world) cities, we also examine, indirectly, the markets and sectors in which London competes. The starting point is to identify sectors where competition with other world cities takes place.

London competes in a number of markets and with a number of world cities:

- Headquarters (control/command functions): New York, Tokyo, Frankfurt and Paris.
- Global financial and business services: New York, Tokyo and Frankfurt.
- Innovation and universities: New York, Paris and Boston.
- Tourism/culture: Paris, New York, Rome, Venice and Prague.
- Retail: Paris, New York and Milan.
- Government: Brussels, Edinburgh and Cardiff.
- Transport: Amsterdam, Paris and Frankfurt.

Because of lack of data availability, and in order to focus discussion, this chapter does not cover all of the above sectors/markets; instead, it will concentrate on the first five areas set out above. Although the above markets are inextricably linked, the first two are perhaps more critically intertwined in economic terms.

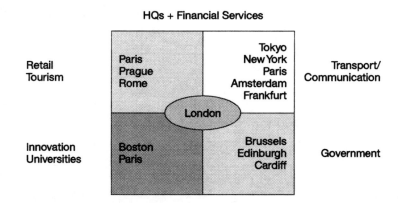

Figure 3.3 London's competitors

Competition in providing HQs

London attracts HQs of the largest corporations, a characteristic of a world city. However, there are other reasons for such a clustering of the global command functions in London and competitive world cities. Scale (in terms of size of population/hinterlands/economy) is combined with a close and productive network of supply, subcontracting and intermediate services and production. Many of these companies are located in the 'City Fringe' area discussed in Chapter 2. Such clustering forms the basis of agglomeration economies. It creates a significant market of itself whose needs must be met, a large pool of human resources and flexible enterprise structure, all of which are crucial to an effective response to the unpredictable demands of global markets.

The size of Tokyo, London and New York implies a dominant role in the national economy as well as the existence of a large market. This in itself, rather than global economic considerations alone, has influenced many domestic and international corporations to base themselves in these cities. In the world city league table, Tokyo has the greatest dominance of its national economy, followed by London, Paris and New York.[8] Frankfurt attracts corporate HQs not because of its size (which is less than one-tenth of London's in population terms), but due to its economic and financial strength in the German economy and its role as an international financial centre.

While the economic life of other cities tends to be based around branches and subsidiaries, London, New York, Frankfurt, Paris and Tokyo accommodate front- and head-office activities of multinational companies as well as international stock markets and/or seats of political power (Berlin – in the past and future, London, Tokyo and Paris). These command elements are important to the status of a world city, not least because they attract further businesses and other economic activity.

It is interesting to note that, unlike London, in New York many corporate HQs have left to move out to the suburbs or even into other states. Although in the recent past the loss in employment has been masked by the growth of financial services, this must be regarded as a significant loss of control and decision-making capacity from the heart of New York.[9] In the case of Germany, the re-establishment of Berlin as a capital city is

---

[8] Llewelyn-Davies et al, *Four World Cities*, GOL (1996).
[9] Corporation of London, *London – New York Study* (2000).

beginning to lead to the migration of HQ functions to that city. It is too early to see how the balance of such financial and HQ functions will eventually come to rest between Berlin and Frankfurt.[10]

Financial services

An efficient financial system is the backbone of a modern economy. National and global economies rely on their financial sectors to facilitate and develop growth in world trade and, in the process, to enhance their standard of living. A November 2001 report by International Financial Services London concluded that 'Net overseas earnings of the financial sector in the United Kingdom reached a new record of £31.2 billion in 1999, an increase of over £1 billion from the revised figure of £30.0 billion for the previous year ... In the first year since the euro was launched, these record figures show that London continues to stake its place as a leading international financial centre. Service earnings at £17.6 billion were the major component of total net overseas earnings. They were up by £2.3 billion from 1998.'

The CEBR suggests that the key determinants of London's pole position in this sector include the lower unit costs of doing business in London. The research suggests that 'The average competitiveness index, based on London = 100, across the seven markets analysed was found to be 117 for New York, 143 for Tokyo, 155 for Paris and 163 for Frankfurt.'[11] London's competitiveness in each market area, according to the CEBR, is

Table 3.1 City financial and business services competitiveness

	Paris	Frankfurt	Tokyo	New York	London
Wholesale banking	111.3	122.7	115.1	107.5	100
Fund management	193.7	274.8	167.6	135.5	100
Securities trading	304.8	226.3	763.8	129.8	100
Foreign exchange	154.1	159.6	170.1	126.2	100
Insurance	111.4	129.3	144.9	142.3	100
Commodities and derivatives	111.6	109.8	141.5	77.3	100
Professional services	97.5	115.4	121.4	101.5	100

Source: CEBR, 1999
Note: Index allows for the scale and scope of the economies

---

[10] See comments in LSFU, *Third Annual Report* (2001).
[11] CEBR, *Two Great Cities*, Corporation of London (1997); and CEBR, *The Competitiveness of London's Financial and Business Services Sector* (1999).

shown in Table 3.1. The smaller the number, the more competitive the city. In most markets London leads.

London has retained its dominance as a global financial centre despite the introduction of the euro, according to figures published in October 2001 by the Bank for International Settlements (BIS).[12] The data, drawing on research by 48 central banks, showed that more than 30 per cent of spot foreign exchange turnover is dealt with in London. This level was virtually unchanged since 1998, when the figures were last collected, and remained the largest share of any centre in the world by far.

Since the advent of the euro in January 1999, observers have been on alert for signs that the new currency has been undermining London's predominance as a financial centre, with business being moved to Frankfurt or Paris. The October 2001 report from BIS provided the clearest evidence that this has not yet happened. In fact, London's slice of currency trading was equal to that of its nearest three rivals, with the United States taking 16 per cent, Japan 9 per cent and Singapore 6 per cent.

There are a number of factors that contribute to higher competitiveness in financial services in London, including the fact that London has large and well-developed companies in the financial services sector; some are likely to get larger in the current wave of mergers and acquisitions, others may become part of US, German or French companies, or those from other countries. It is likely that British companies will win business away from smaller, less-developed companies in other countries. Recent events (relating to the Eurobond market) suggest that even if British companies lose business to other European companies, they may gain overall market share.

The benefits of size are especially important in the financial services sector. This, together with the dominance of London as an international financial centre, provides economies of scale and scope for London firms despite relatively higher costs (of certain inputs) compared to other centres such as Paris and Frankfurt. Large companies have the economic power to move markets and set their prices, with the result that business tends to gravitate towards them. The existence of the economies of scale and scope greatly boosts British companies' productivity. Economies of scope accrue to firms from linkages (synergies) between the different (financial and business services) markets concentrated in central London.

---

[12] Bank for International Settlements, 2001, *Central Banks Survey* (October 2001).

There are also Central London-specific factors that make London more competitive. International and national factors and those associated with size are reinforced by the many advantages associated with agglomeration economies, which Central London offers to companies in the financial and business services sector. Having developed a (large) critical mass of companies in the financial and business services sector, Central London provides externalities of a magnitude which other (rival) international financial centres cannot – this is reflected in the comparative advantage that London has over other centres. The cost of labour (except for Paris and Frankfurt) and property (except for Tokyo) is higher in London,[13] but the highly advanced telecommunications infrastructure is much more reasonably priced and, as noted above, the average unit cost of doing business in London is lower. London also boasts a large pool of highly skilled labour not only in the financial sector but also in supporting services such as IT consultancy and R&D.

Other 'non-cost' strengths of London include English as an international language, a low level of (personal and corporate) taxation, and the availability of markets which are liquid, efficient and transparent. London markets are large and lightly regulated. Under this scenario, it can be assumed that for the foreseeable future, London's large size makes it difficult for other centres, including Paris and Frankfurt, to compete.

London will continue to attract 'innovating outsiders' as it always has done, thus helping to replace old practices, improve productivity and introduce new products. As Drucker (*The Economist*, September 1999) has remarked, 'This is basically what happened to the old London "City" 35 years ago. Except for Rothschild and Schroders, not one of the leading City firms of 1950–60 is still in English hands, not even Warburg. All have become wholly owned subsidiaries of foreign firms: American, Dutch, Swiss, German, French.' The net result has been increased output and productivity.

London will continue to provide the skilled workforce capable of innovation and efficient use of ICT. On this point, the deregulation of

---

[13] International comparisons on rent are as important, if not more so, because London as a 'world city' competes with other major international cities in terms of location. A Winter 1999 Richard Ellis 'World Office Rents' report suggested that Tokyo ranks at the top for overall occupation costs of office space followed by Hong Kong, and London takes third position. It is important to make a couple of points here. First, London's competitiveness as an international location has improved markedly since the late 1980s. Second, London is high up on total occupation costs mainly because the burden of taxation is one of the highest in the world. If a comparison of net rent was taken, London would compare favourably with other major European cities such as Paris, Frankfurt and Berlin.

ICT is not envisaged in the foreseeable future and this has important implications for London. Although technology makes it easier to relocate, it nevertheless can centralise rather than decentralise trade (including within the financial and business services sector). The many advantages of London's telecommunications infrastructure mean that it is well placed to benefit, rather than suffer, from the globalisation of markets.

Other assumptions underpinning this scenario include:

- maintaining the provision of a large, competitive, skilled labour force for central London economic activities;
- making the best of English being the international language of business and commerce;
- enhancing London's world-class telecommunications infrastructure;
- maintaining a liberal regulatory environment;
- maintaining a low level of taxation;
- fostering London's high share of overseas lending;
- fostering productivity gains made recently in the financial and business services sector;
- exploiting to the full the economies of scale and scope.

Finally, it is likely that the United Kingdom will enter the European Monetary Union (EMU) during the next 10 years, which will further encourage London's financial sector.

Business services, ICT and the creative industries: convergence and diversification

All the world cities are characterised by a dynamic diversity of economic activity. A broad spectrum of business activity enables them to exploit effectively a diversity of opportunities, to respond flexibly and efficiently to competitive threats, and to some extent insulate themselves against shocks and tribulations of the national and global economy. What is important is the existence of dynamic diversity in those areas of economic, social and political activities that benefit from urban agglomeration economies. These economies also provide the capacity for creativity and innovation, which are needed to survive.

Creativity and innovation and the factors that promote them are extremely difficult to identify and measure. They can be recognised only when they can be applauded. For example, the highly innovative character of London's financial sector is exemplified by its successful development of the Eurobond market. Innovation and creativity will be discussed in due course with tourism, below; for the moment, the theme of command and creativity will be illustrated by examining in more detail the wealth creation capabilities in the financial services and cultural sectors relative to other world cities.

In both London and New York the globalisation of business services and at the same time the sector links into the wider pool of creative industries are apparent. Both cities have global companies in accounting, legal services and above all advertising. These services draw on other services in more routine occupations that are often located further out from the main business centre (ie Manhattan/the City). Both cities have profited from their strengths in ICT and telecommunications to develop influential communities of small New Media companies that have developed new products around recent technological and multimedia developments. In both London (Soho, Hoxton) and New York ('Silicon Alley', Chelsea, Garment District) particular clusters of New Media companies have achieved an international reputation.[14]

The character of these developments in another of London's competitors in this area – Paris – has been rather different. Paris shares with London and New York a very strong creative and artistic tradition (eg fashion, and music) that filters into service sector occupations, but its history in ICT development has been different. France developed its own very successful 'on-line' information system, Minitel, in the 1980s. Evidence from the 2000/2001 Paris–London Employer Survey suggests that businesses in London and Paris make use of on-line services for different activities. Companies in London are more likely to use the Internet for e-commerce. Companies in Paris are more likely to use the Internet for research. The debate about the take-up of the Internet in France is also linked to the debate about the extent of use of the French language in IT.[15]

---

[14] For these developments, see the London–New York study, *op cit*, note 6, as well as various London studies concerned with the 'City Fringe' area as discussed here in Chapter 3. Also LSFU, *Creative Skills* (2000) on New Media in London and its integration with other business services.

[15] See LSFU/OFEM, *Les Villes Apprenantes/Learning Cities* (2001).

In summary, business services, ICT and creative industries have become closely linked in global city functions. It is the pool of creativity and diversity business services within global cities that supports major international service industry companies. For London it is apparent that the links between the City, business services in the City Fringe and the creative industries will provide a major element of the capital's future competitiveness.

Innovation and R&D

A key aspect of competitiveness is the degree to which companies innovate. Innovation can include the introduction of new business processes or new products.

Traditionally, the degree of innovation has been measured by the amount of spending undertaken on R&D. For countries, this spend can then be assessed as a proportion of overall production (GDP). During the 1990s' economic boom, the US level of innovation raced away from that of the United Kingdom and other EU countries. The proportion of UK GDP spent on R&D was above the European average for most of the 1990s but fell below this level in 1997 and 1998.

When examined at regional level within Europe, the position of London is even worse. Although London ranks seventh in its overall level of production in Europe, it ranks below all its major competitors by proportion of GDP spent on R&D. When European capital regions are considered, it is behind Ile-de-France (Paris), Berlin, Lombardia (Milan) and Lazio (Rome). Ile-de-France was the region in Europe with the largest proportion of the workforce in research and the largest overall expenditure on R&D.[16]

Another European study suggests that in both manufacturing and services London has only average proportions of employers who have introduced new products or services. In manufacturing, 51 per cent of London employers carried out such innovations, compared with 59 per cent for the United Kingdom and 53 per cent for the European Union as a whole. In services, the London figure was 49 per cent compared to 40 per cent for the United Kingdom and 41 per cent for Europe.[17]

---

[16] I Laafia, *R&D expenditure and personnel in Europe and its regions,* Eurostat (2001).
[17] EU Community Innovation Survey.

Naturally, as stated at the beginning of this section, innovation does not consist solely in expenditure on new product development. Development of new services or business processes can be equally important in improving competitiveness by increasing efficiency or quality of service to the customer. Some comparison of the level of this impact in London and Paris can be obtained from the 1999 employer surveys conducted by LSFU, and by the Regional Chamber of Commerce of Ile-de-France. Although the questions asked in the two surveys are not precisely the same, they nevertheless suggest that by this definition the overall level of innovation was similar in both cities.

Tourism

Tourism is generally considered to be one of the fastest expanding industries around the world. Cheaper international travel is encouraging leisure tourist trips, while globalisation is encouraging more frequent business travel.

The London New York study undertook a pioneering, if brief, common assessment of visitors in both cities.[18] It proved difficult to reach a common definition on domestic visitors. There was, however, a clear contrast in international visitor numbers between the two cities. The number of international visits (for business or leisure) was substantially higher in London and increased markedly in the mid-1990s. By contrast,

Table 3.2 Innovation by companies in Paris and London

Sector	London (percentage of companies introducing new products or services in the last three years)	Paris (percentage of companies suggesting that new products or services have had an impact on the organisation)
Manufacturing	51	41
Construction	20	40
Transport	50	55
Retail	51	53
Services	45	53
Total	45	48

Source: London Employer Survey, 1999; CRCI Ile-de-France Référence Emploi Formation, 1999

---

[18] *London New York Study, op cit,* note 6, pp 83–112.

international visitor numbers to New York have increased only slightly during the same period. Spending by international visitors in 1998 was estimated at £6.73 billion and US$6.1 billion respectively.

The study concluded that London had the advantage of:

- close proximity to an international market;
- a better 'heritage' offer;
- closer government involvement in tourism policy and investment.

Crime and local transport were seen as negatives for both cities.[19]

Paris was the 'most visited city in the world' according to international tourism sources. The Four World Cities Study of 1996 found that in the early 1990s Paris received 11 million international visitors per year compared to 11.5 million in London, 5.5 million in New York and 2.3 million in Tokyo. The Paris figures only included hotel stays and were thus underestimates. London and Paris saw similar, lower levels of domestic tourism at around 9 million domestic visitors, while New York and Tokyo had higher levels of around 20 million domestic visitors.[20]

The 1996 World City report also provides a due warning about the extent to which the cities compete for international tourism, since they

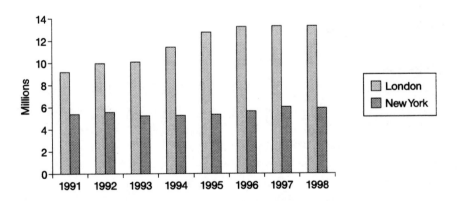

Source: London–New York Study (2000), after LTB and NYCVB

Figure 3.4 International visitors to London and New York, 1991–1998

---

[19] In 2001, Paris' image was strongly affected by a major increase in petty street crime, resulting in much comment in the international media.
[20] Llewelyn-Davies et al, *op cit*, note X, Table 5.1, p 130.

each have particular appeals to particular markets. Thus, Paris has a readier market than London for short breaks by those living on the Continent. The London–New York study also suggests that New York has a large market within North America, though it also sees heavy competition from destinations such as Florida.

The attacks on the World Trade Center in New York on 11 September 2001 have had a catastrophic effect on a British tourist industry already suffering from the effects of BSE and foot-and-mouth. Even before the attacks, the London Tourist Board estimated that visitor numbers were down by between 9 and 14 per cent. Nevertheless, it is clear that in the longer term the industry is set for continued global expansion, perhaps not in 2002, but by 2003 London will have to consider carefully its strategy for maintaining its competitiveness in such a major source of foreign currency.

Retailing

Analysis of the 1998 London Employer Survey (Table 1.4) suggested that 12,000 jobs, or less than 1 per cent of retail employment in London, depended on overseas markets. These jobs are heavily concentrated in Central London, where many retailers have the potential to generate considerable revenue from foreign visitors. A study for LSFU by Cambridge Econometrics concluded that training for retail staff to deal with foreign customers had considerable scope for creating further growth in income, much more than for domestic customers.

The familiarity to Londoners of major shops in Paris (Galeries Lafayette, Printemps) and New York (Bloomingdales, Maceys) testifies to the degree to which these cities can compete directly with London. The outcry in Paris at the closure announcement of their branch of Marks & Spencer demonstrates the feelings that can be generated. Such major retailers are concentrated in equally well-known tourist hotspots, which help to reinforce their position in international markets – Knightsbridge, Oxford Street, Grand Boulevards and Opera.

Key elements of London's competitiveness

This chapter has defined competitiveness in terms of the capacity of a city's businesses to meet customer needs in various contested markets as well as the city's capacity to meet the economic, social and physical needs of its population and workers.

An analysis by Londonomics Ltd of weighted indicators of competitiveness for London suggests that the weights given by the business community to the 'labour components' of London's competitiveness are higher than those given to other components – for example, the 'transport infrastructure component'. Brauerhjelm[21] suggests that the essential components of a successful European regional policy include a skilled and educated workforce: 'This is important not just because skilled workers are more productive, but also because better educated workers can benefit more from the transfer of know-how between firms that takes place in local agglomeration. They are also more mobile and more likely to shift from low- to high-yield activities.'

The LSFU and reports by two London TECs[22] have demonstrated that ICT skills are of major importance to (knowledge-driven) London employers and employees; a skills shortage has adverse effects on output, productivity, investment plans and, by implication, competitiveness. Information technology is becoming a defining feature of the London economy. Computer literacy is becoming a basic skill requirement that people must have to meet the demand for more knowledge workers.

Table 3.3 (page 77) provides the results of weighting London's competitiveness indicators, showing the relative importance of each indicator in the overall competitiveness of London. Clustered under four aggregate components of (London) competitiveness (with a total weighting ratio of 1.00, the third column in Table 3.3), the 'demand conditions' are most important, assuming a weighting of 0.34, followed by the 'input/supply conditions' 0.27, the 'supporting conditions' 0.23, and finally (business/ city) 'management conditions' have a weighting of 0.16.

The results, presented in a Porterian formulation of competitiveness components, appear to be similar (at the aggregate level) to those arrived at by INTER/VIEW for 10 European world cities.[23] INTER/VIEW uses 14 indicators, which are more pertinent to business (than urban) competitiveness. INTER/VIEW's work showed that the demand and supply

---

21 P Brauerhjelm et al, *Integration and Regions of Europe: How the right practice can prevent polarisation*, CEPR (2000).

22 LSFU, *Second Annual Report* (2000), WLTEC, *IT Skills into the Twenty-First Century* (1999), and Focus Central London, *IT Skills, Needs and Training Provision in Central London* (1999).

23 INTER/VIEW, *The Competitive Advantage of Ten Major Cities in Europe* (1992).

conditions scored higher than the other two conditions of competitiveness. In an urban competitiveness context, and using 24 indicators which reflect both business/city performance, the results also show that the demand and supply conditions assume supremacy over the other two conditions.

Within the 'demand conditions', productivity (of labour) and level of demand score the highest, ranked 5 and 6 respectively. Under the 'input/supply conditions', the availability of labour and transport infrastructure score highest, ranked 1 and 4 respectively. Quality of telecommunications (ranked 2) and education and infrastructure (ranked 3) are strong attributes of the 'supporting condition'. Finally, the strongest indicators under 'management conditions' are, respectively, perceptions of business about the future of the city (ranked 7), reflecting a degree of certainty, or otherwise, for future investment, and quality of life (ranked 8).

In overall terms, the five indicators of urban competitiveness which rank highest in the list of 24 indicators used in this study respectively are:

- availability of skilled workers;
- quality of telecommunications infrastructure;
- education and training infrastructure;
- transport infrastructure;
- productivity (of labour).

In spite of the fact that the results are based on an admittedly small sample of London-based businesses, the results are (as noted above) remarkably consistent with other surveys – for example, the London Chamber of Commerce and Industry's foreign banking survey and Healey & Baker's European Cities Monitor. The results are also supported by an analysis of the financial statements of 50 randomly chosen London-based HQs[24] and also by our analysis of the UK Input-Output table.

As Table 3.3 shows, the LCCI's survey of London-based foreign banks also shows that the 'weight' given to availability of labour is highest, followed by quality. As expected, the foreign banking community places emphasis on the depth of the financial markets and the tradition of London as an international financial centre, both scoring high, at 6.6 and 6.4 respectively (on a ratio of 100).

---

[24] In terms of turnover, the range was £5.1 million, the smallest, to £4,117 million, the largest. Employment ranges from 20 people in small firms to 38,656 people in large firms.

Table 3.3 Weighted indicators of London's competitiveness

Indicator	Londonomics' Key Components of Urban Competitiveness	Weights	Londonomics' indicators of Urban Competitiveness	Finance Directors' Survey-based (June/July 2000) weights	Rank	Comparable LCCI's (April 2000) weights	Comparable H&B's (August 1999) weights
1	Demand Conditions	0.34	Per capita GDP (level + rate of change)	2.9	18	na	na
2			Productivity (GDP per worker: level/rate of change)	4.8	5	na	na
3			Employment (level + rate of change)	4.4	9	na	na
4			R&D spend (% of GDP)	2.9	18	na	na
5			Forex turnover (daily – $ billion)	3.4	16	na	na
6			International air travel (no. of passengers per year)	4.2	11	3.8	10.3
7			Number of tourists visiting the city	3.4	16	na	na
8			% of people of working age in employment	4.0	12	na	na
9			Level of client demand (size of the market)	4.7	6	5.4	na
10	Input/Supply Conditions	0.27	Availability of skilled workers (business perception)	6.5	1	7.1	7.7
11			Office occupational costs	3.5	15	4.7	4.5
12			Average earnings per hour	2.8	19	4.3	7.7
13			Labour unit cost	4.5	8	4.3	na
14			Unemployment	4.0	12	na	na
15			Transport (infrastructure/stress on roads)	5.2	4	4.3	3.2
16	Supporting Conditions	0.23	Education and training infrastructure	5.4	3	2.8	na
17			Quality of telecommunications infrastructure	5.7	2	6.7	9.2
18			Government support to business (regulation/taxation)	3.6	14	4.7	6.7
19			Quality of supply chain	3.3	17	na	na
20			Level of creativity/innovation (business/Government)	4.3	10	na	na
21	Management Conditions	0.16	Promotion: city-wide policy/effectiveness	3.6	14	na	na
22			Perceptions of business about future of city	4.6	7	na	na
23			Crime rate (% change over time)	3.8	13	na	na
24			Quality of Life (pollution, green space)	4.5	8	3.5	2
	TOTAL	1.00		100.0			

Source: Londonomics Ltd, July 2000, *London's Competitiveness Index – Weighting the Indicators. (A report prepared for LSFU.)*

In the case of the Healey & Baker survey, easy access to markets and proximity to competitors (both indicators of demand) score highest at 11.2 (on a ratio of 100). International air transport scores higher in the Healey & Baker survey compared with LCCI's or our own survey. This is perhaps because of the nature of the survey sample; most of the respondents being located in Europe would, expectedly, place high emphasis on international links to facilitate (physical) access to business locations. It is important to note, however, that the international business community gives considerable weight to the availability of labour and cost of labour in their business operations. Finally, it is interesting to note that in both Healey & Baker's and our own surveys, the perception about the future of the city is a significant consideration in urban competitiveness terms. This provides an indication of certainty for the business community – an important consideration in any investment decision.

Our analysis of the financial statements of 50 London-based HQs suggests that the cost of labour, relative to total 'cost of doing business'/'cost of sales', ranges from 10.8 per cent in the case of some manufacturing firms to 66.1 per cent in the case of companies in the financial and business services sector. On average, labour costs are around the 50 per cent mark of total costs of 'inputs'. This suggests that labour is important in the process of production/delivery of goods and services, and therefore it validates the high 'weights' assigned to availability and skills of labour by MDs and finance directors. In contrast, transport costs were generally low (at around 4–5 per cent) as a proportion of total 'inputs' costs. In some cases (eg the aerospace sector), transport costs were as high as 11.8 per cent. This is perhaps part of the explanation for the 'transport infrastructure' indicator scoring lower than telecommunications or availability of labour.

These results are identical to the results of our analysis of the 1998 UK Input-Output tables, which shed light on costs of 'inputs' in various sectors of the economy. Wages and salaries as a proportion of total input range from 24.1 per cent in the agriculture sector to 58.0 per cent in public administration/health sectors of the economy. This supports, yet again, the proposition that, generally, the labour input is very significant.

The above analysis might be seen to have 'proven the obvious' – in other words, the labour input is important in the context of competitiveness. This might well be the case, but this message has been accentuated in the three business surveys analysed above. More to the point, the above analysis which shows a significantly higher, relative importance of labour in the overall competitiveness index has, in turn, significant policy implications for London's future performance.

If all the labour-related indicators[25] were added together, their aggregate weight would be much larger than that of any other indicator of competitiveness (16.7 out of a total of 100). This ought to send a powerful message to policy makers in London and nationally about the importance of skills and training. There is nothing 'revolutionary' about this finding. However, the LSFU study simply provides new quantitative evidence in a competitiveness context, which meaningfully accentuates the tremendous importance of skills and people in delivering higher and higher business/city competitiveness.

International productivity: London and Paris

Productivity is a key aspect of competitiveness. It is closely related to industrial efficiency and the levels of skills in the workforce. Chapter 2 showed how the US boom in the 1990s was driven by productivity improvements, while in Chapter 6 academic research is cited to suggest that the United Kingdom is in a 'low-skills equilibrium' competing at an international level on price of goods rather than productivity and quality. One of the current British government's primary aims is to increase productivity.

The CEBR 1997 study of Paris and London conducted a considerable amount of comparative econometric analysis of productivity, based on re-examination of GDP figures for the two regions. It adjusted GDP to account for national differentials in production, different levels of commuting in the two regions and different national systems of accounting for interest payment of foreign banks (a significant element of both cities' 'production' given their role as global financial centres). The conclusion was that London's productivity was 28 per cent higher than the rest of the United Kingdom, whereas the productivity of workers in Ile-de-France (the Paris region) was only 21 per cent higher than in the rest of France. In other words, while at national level France's productivity

---

[25] That is, productivity, availability of skilled labour, education and training infrastructure, excluding employment, economic participation (percentage of people of working age in employment), average earnings and labour cost.

was higher than that of the United Kingdom, when the two capitals were compared London has a higher level of productivity in relation to the United Kingdom than Paris has in relation to France.[26]

Two implications of this work are:

- Further work is needed to set London and its competitors within a comparable economic context.
- Although much needs to be done to increase UK productivity, London workers are well placed to compete with other capital regions.

The second point bears out the great strides in London's manufacturing productivity set out in Chapter 1, in addition to the importance of the London workforce for London's competitiveness, which has been set out in this chapter.

London as part of a global labour market

As a great capital city London is not only part of the global economic system, but is also part of the global communications system. Two of its airports – Heathrow and Gatwick – are among the busiest in the world. The huge range of international businesses in the city is responsible for bringing in large numbers of foreign business people as workers and clients. Indeed, Heathrow regularly has to cope with people who interrupt flights around the globe for a quick meeting in London! Apart from foreign workers and business visitors, there is therefore a range of people every day who dip in and out of the London economy, as it were, on their way across the globe.

Another part of the global movement in which London is engaged applies at the bottom edge of the economic scale – refugees. Because of London's place as a capital, and as the location of the main entry points into the United Kingdom, London tends to accommodate over half of all refugees entering the country. This movement is encouraged by the cosmopolitan nature of London's population, including over half of all the United Kingdom's ethnic minorities. Refugees who come to London are

---

[26]   CEBR, *Two Great Cities*, Corporation of London (1997), Chapter 3.

thus more likely to find people from their own community who can ease their transition into a new country.

When considering global communications in terms of people, it is easy to overlook the global exchange of information via telecommunications which forms the lifeblood of London's businesses. London is a global centre for broadcasting and communications, as a few examples can demonstrate:

- Reuters provides a worldwide network of news agency and financial data.
- The BBC is renowned for its international public broadcasts.
- East London is a major hub in the Internet, switching and packaging electronic information around the world.

London is therefore a strong centre where businesses can both obtain the global information they need to do business and distribute their information to customers or suppliers.

London is not simply part of a global market in terms of business, but is part of a global market for labour. People come to London as part of international companies or as refugees. Citizens of any EU country can and do work in London at all levels of occupation. Citizens of non-EU countries also find employment in London in large numbers, as witnessed by the recent employment of teachers from Eastern Europe and Asia to meet shortages in London schools.

London can therefore increasingly find itself in direct competition for key workers in other global cities. European legislation is explicitly designed to encourage labour movement in this regard. New York has always been a 'mecca' for immigrants and there are signs that there, as in London, there is a growing appreciation that the education system has to equip residents with the skills to enable them to compete in this global market.[27] In London, as Chapter 5 explains, this competition with non-residents starts to happen at the level of tertiary education (NVQ Level 3). It is important to realise that, increasingly, we are not simply talking about the competitiveness of London as a business environment and London businesses as competitive on the global scale, but instead we need to consider the competitiveness of Londoners in an international

---

[27] *London–New York Study, op cit*, note 6, p 33.

job market. Naturally, this is less likely to apply for lower-level occupations and qualifications, but few occupations are completely immune to such pressures.

Education and training

The workforce and those people seeking work in world cities provide the supply of skills to the labour markets. They will have acquired their skills in a mix of educational institutions, training facilities and companies or other employing organisations based in the city, elsewhere in the country or even abroad. The national education and training infrastructure is therefore essential to the supply of skills to London, Paris and Berlin, etc. However, the extent to which the city reflects or contains more of the national system's strengths or weaknesses will play an important role in determining the city's competitiveness both in global terms and as a location for national and international business. Recently, a 1999 report entitled 'The Skills Challenge' by the US Council on Competitiveness has singled out 'worker skills as the greatest competitive challenge the nation faces over the next decade'. Their concern reflects broad recognition among leaders from business and universities that the United States faces 'compelling pressures to upgrade the US skills base'.

Earlier, Porter provided a useful framework for assessing the education and training infrastructure's role in sustaining competitive advantage. He concluded that 'advanced' and 'specialist' skills provided a stronger base for sustainable competitive advantage than skills, which could be defined as 'basic' or 'generalised'. This was simply because the latter are more easily replicable elsewhere. For this reason – the ready transferability of skills – the private sector was less likely to be interested in risking their investment in such skills. Private sector investment in advanced and specialist skills was both more integral to competitive advantage and less easily transferable, and therefore investment in such skills was more necessary, desirable and likely.

This section will concentrate on international comparisons of education and training. Data limitations will constrain what can be reported. It will then consider whether London has any marked deficiencies or strengths relative to its competitor cities. Where such comparisons do not exist, it will use national figures as proxy.

Recent OECD figures (Economic Survey, 1999) on youth participation rates[28] in education and training suggest that the United Kingdom is on a par with France and Germany, but below the United States and Japan. However, analysis by benchmarking against UNESCO's ISCED international qualification framework suggests that the United States and United Kingdom have a considerable deficit in intermediate qualifications compared to European countries (particularly Scandinavia and Germany).[29] It is possible that this is because of a high dropout rate in UK further education institutions, but it should then be considered whether those dropping out have already acquired the skills they need. Chapter 5 discusses aspects of the distinction between skills and qualifications. The profile of qualifications presented in Chapter 5 also suggests that London has a higher level of intermediate qualifications (Level 3) than other regions of the United Kingdom (Table 5.21, page 132).

The large number of further and higher education institutions give London a distinct edge compared to many other regions, and the Londonomics competitiveness index suggests that the presence of a highly qualified labour force was one of the factors that companies most valued about London. Chapter 5 will demonstrate how London out-performs the National Learning Targets on several counts. It may perhaps be no surprise therefore to find that the European Labour Force Survey suggests that Inner London has the highest proportion of the workforce with degrees of any European region.[30] This high level of qualification was closely mirrored by those of the home counties. It was also noted that the Ile-de-France region around Paris had a comparatively low level of degree-level qualifications, similar to some of the more remote areas of France. It was tentatively suggested that this difference could be explained by the high percentages of students moving to London to study and then staying on to enter the workforce rather than returning to their original homes. Further impacts of this movement of students are discussed in Chapters 5 and 6.

Chapter 6 emphasises how London's economy is more volatile than that of south east England, leading to persistence in unemployment. The

---

[28] The number of 16–19 year olds in higher education per 100,000 inhabitants.

[29] See A Green and H Steedman (1997), *Into the Twenty First Century: an assessment of British skill profiles and prospects*, CEP London School of Economics (1997) and P Brown, A Green and H Lauder, *High Skills, Globalization, Competitiveness and Skill Formation*, Oxford (2001).

[30] S Pilos, *Education in the Regions of the European Union*, Eurostat (2001). CEBR, *op cit*, note X, pp 72–6, though noting the higher qualifications in Ile-de-France than in France does not fully assess its position in relation to other regions of the country.

Paris region is also more volatile than the rest of France. The CEBR suggests that London is more volatile in relation to the United Kingdom than Paris is to France, and that this differential pattern of growth could impact on training.[31] Further work is required to consider how this 'over volatility' of both regions can be related to the variability of regional levels of qualification shown in Figure 3.5.

It may be argued that with regard to competitiveness, the degree to which employers commit to training for employees is of great significance Furthermore, to the extent that London is competing with other world cities, the comparative level of training provided in different cities is also significant.

Since 1997, the LSFU has been exchanging data from their annual surveys of employers for similar data collected by the Regional Chamber of Commerce of Ile-de-France and the Paris Chamber of Commerce. Although there is a compulsory training levy on all French companies, a consistent trend has been observed in which London companies are more likely to provide training to their employees. More detailed analysis based on a joint Paris–London survey in 2001 using exactly the same question-naire in both cities has demonstrated that the key difference is that London companies with between 10 and 49 employees are more likely to

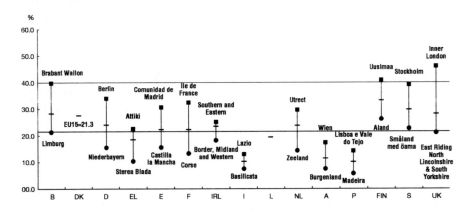

Source: S Pilos, Eurostat, 2001

Figure 3.5 Percentage of adults with a tertiary education qualification at national level and regional extremes, 1999

---

31 CEBR, *op cit, note X*, p 66, relating business cycles 'sur-productivity' and endogenous growth.

provide training.[32] This evidence supports the suggestion in Chapter 5 that UK SMEs are more likely to provide training than their EU counterparts.

The overall rate of training provision by companies in Berlin is 21 per cent, much lower than either London or Paris. However, this figure does not include the high proportion of German companies that invest directly in further education colleges – a salutary lesson in the difficulties of international comparisons![33]

Conclusion

In 2000–2001, the LSFU in conjunction with the Skills Observatory (OFEM) of the Paris Chamber of Commerce carried out exactly the same survey in London and Paris.[34] Analysis looked at differences in company performance within and between the cities. It was hypothesised, for

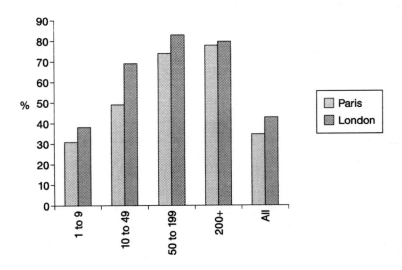

Source: London Employer Survey/Paris Chamber of Commerce Survey, 2001

Figure 3.6 Companies providing training by numbers employed in Paris and London, 2001

32   LSFU OFEM, *Les Villes Apprenantes – Learning Cities* (2001).
33   LSFU, *Third Annual Report* (2001) pp 40–1, following SOSTRA, *Betriebspanel Berlin 1999* (2000).
34   LSFU OFEM, *Les Villes Apprenantes/Learning Cities* (2001).

example, that globalisation might lead to large companies in both cities having more similar behaviour than small companies. In fact, it proved that there was much more variation in the performance of different sectors and sizes of company within each city than there was between the two cities.

This leads back to the gist of our definition of competitiveness (page 62). It is *companies* that compete with each other. Regions compete in the sense that they provide a conducive environment and the infrastructure that helps individual companies to compete and thrive. This chapter has suggested that the 'cost of doing business' in London is lower than its competitors. The Londonomics work, supported by other studies, has proved that the quality of London's labour force is fundamental in this regard.

The conventional picture of London's international reputation built on the financial might of the City has been reinforced by this analysis. At the same time, however, it has been shown how the creativity, dynamism and breadth of London's service industries, linked to the firm foundation of the national economy, help to create a strong base for London's future growth.

Finally, the key point that appears to emerge from the above analysis is that London does attract the highly skilled and innovators. This will continue to provide a conducive environment to keep itself in pole position as a global financial and business centre.

4

Commuters and Residents

Introduction

For the majority of people working in the United Kingdom, travelling to work means taking a short journey by car or public transport. Home and work place are both located within the same district council area. In London, however, travelling to work can mean a long journey, crossing into a different borough, or moving from outside London into the centre of the capital.

Travel to work patterns in London are complex. On average, about 50 per cent of people live in the borough in which they work, a proportion which is generally higher for outlying boroughs and lower for those in the centre, particularly the City, which has a small resident population and a huge influx of workers. The daily 'tide' of commuters into London both in the morning and out again in the evening lends a particular character to London's economy.

To analyse travel to work patterns in London we rely on administrative boundaries, usually boroughs or definitions of 'London' and 'not London'. On the ground, these definitions may be fairly meaningless: if a person lives just outside London and works in one of the outlying boroughs, this could actually be a shorter journey to work than for a person who travels to work from, for example, Enfield in the north to Croydon in the south, or from Hounslow in the west to Dagenham in the east.

These long journeys and large numbers of people moving between areas create many tensions. Some parts of London have completely different populations in the day and at night, as workers disappear home and residents return. The City has two large non-resident populations as cleaners and service staff replace daytime workers at night. These two groups pass each other in the early morning going in opposite directions – one to work and the other to home. Those going to work are among the most affluent groups in London; those going home are among the poorest.

Public transport infrastructure, roads and rail lines have to cope with huge volumes of movement. People looking for a job within their borough may have to compete for jobs with people coming from outside London. During their lives, Londoners may live in different parts of the city, or live in the countryside beyond, while not moving their place of work by less than a mile.

This chapter seeks to set out some of the reasons for these flows of people and the tensions they create. The difficulties of transport and housing in London have been the subject of widespread public debate. This debate is outside the scope of this book, however, as it covers a wide range of very complex technical and policy issues. Transport and housing help to form the infrastructure on which the London economy is founded. We are interested in transport as a significant factor in moving workers and as a means of moving goods; we are less concerned with the mode of transport (car, bus, train etc) or with the capacity of particular routes, the investment required to meet future demand etc. These issues should be left instead to specialists in these subjects.

Levels and patterns of commuting

In excess of one million people commute into Central London every day. The level of commuting rose during the 1980s, fell after 1988 due to the recession, but began to rise again after 1992 (Figure 4.1).

In 1999 and 2000, the London Skills Survey asked people about where they worked and lived. In both years, the proportion of commuters was about the same, with approximately one in every seven workers commuting into London to work.

As would be expected, the majority of commuters into London (91 per cent) actually live in the two adjacent regions – the South East (where 51 per cent of all incoming London commuters live) and the eastern region (41 per cent). Within these regions there are a number of counties that are of particular importance. In the South East, Surrey is the home residence of 19 per cent of all incoming commuters, and Kent 15 per cent. In the

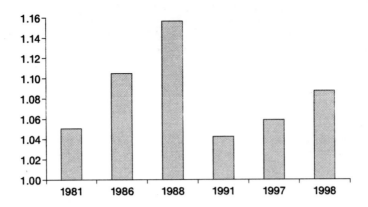

Source: Transport for London

Figure 4.1 Numbers of people commuting into Central London (millions)

eastern region, Essex is the home of 25 per cent of all London in-commuters, with Hertfordshire being the home of a further 13 per cent. There is some evidence of long-distance commuting, which often receives wide publicity, but in reality these constitute only a tiny proportion of all commuters and an even smaller proportion of the overall workforce.

Migration and commuting

Classifying people as 'commuters' and 'non-commuters' implies that the two states are static, that once a commuter always a commuter or, alternatively, once living in London people will always stay there. This is patently not true as people move both jobs and homes. The reasons for moving are

Table 4.1 Proportions of employed people in London who are resident or commuters

	1999	2000
	%	%
Live in London	87	86
Live outside London	13	14
Base	9,806	6,768

Source: London Skills Surveys, 1999 and 2000

Table 4.2 Place of residence of people working in London, 1999

	All employed people %	Commuters %
Live in London	87	–
Live outside London	13	100
South East	6	51
Berkshire	1	5
Buckinghamshire	1	5
Hampshire	–	2
Kent	2	15
Oxfordshire	–	1
Surrey	2	19
Sussex	1	5
Eastern	5	41
Bedfordshire	–	2
Cambridgeshire	–	1
Essex	2	25
Hertfordshire	2	13
South West	–	1
East Midlands	–	1
Leicestershire	–	1
Northamptonshire	–	1
West Midlands	–	–
North, North West and Yorkshire and Humber	–	2
Cheshire	–	2
Lancashire	–	1
Yorkshire	–	1
Other	–	3
Sample base	*9,806*	*1,238*

Source: London Skills Survey, 1999
Note: Only counties with at least 1 per cent of commuters shown

varied and complex, relating to housing opportunities, job opportunities, quality of life and family formation.

Long-distance migrants are often motivated by employment. Thus, a large proportion of people moving to London and the South East from beyond these regions do so to take up employment. Where they decide to live when they arrive in London and the South East will depend as much on non-economic factors such as lifestyle and housing availability.

The 'traditional' pattern for Londoners is that people live in Central London when relatively young and then move out as they get older, form relationships and have children. These moves are related to housing needs (often the need for more accommodation) or environment, and are undertaken without any regard to employment opportunities, present or future. This leads to a period of extended commuting until in the course of time an appropriate local job opportunity comes to their attention.

Few short-distance moves within London and its commuting belt are motivated by job opportunities. Given a desirable lifestyle, a firm group of friends and a good environment (in other words, all things being equal), it is always possible to commute across London to work.

Such moves have been modelled[1] and one of the most dominant features is environmental preference. That is, people move because they prefer the area in which they live to that in which they work and are willing to put up with the cost and inconvenience of commuting. This gives us some difficulty, as measures of environmental quality are intrinsically problematic, and bound up with value judgements. However, the majority of people clearly prefer semi-rural middle-class environments to major cities.

It is important to distinguish between two movements. The first is the propensity for Londoners, particularly after starting a family, to move out of London in search of a better environment – migration. The second is the ability of people living at an increasing distance from London to compete for high-income jobs in the capital without needing to move house – commuting. The two movements are complementary and closely related to transport questions. The migration of a number of London families to a particular part of the Home Counties can encourage local residents to consider working in London. Equally, the growth of a significant number of people from a particular town, who work in London, can encourage those living in London to move out to that town.

Throughout the period from the early 1960s to the early 1980s, approximately one million residents left London every year. Since 1984, however, the level of out-migration has fallen, such that when combined with new births and in-migration, the overall population has risen. In the late 1990s, London has experienced an annual net gain in population (moves into London were more numerous than moves out) from all except the southern regions of the United Kingdom (South East, South West, Eastern).

---

[1]   See, for example, I R Gordon, 'A long-term perspective on inter-regional migration', *Regional Economic Prospects*, July 1999.

As previously suggested, migration has, however, been heavily influenced by social factors. In-migrants to London are more likely to be younger people, including students in particular. The movement of people to study in London can be seen as a 'temporary' phenomenon that will be reversed on graduation. However, there is a heavy 'leakage' as those studying in London stay on to take up work. In 2000, some 48 per cent of higher education students studying in London were prior residents in the capital, whereas 71 per cent of those studying in London took up their first jobs there.[2] Graduates whose home is in London thus also face competition from those from outside London.

Out-migrants are likely to be families with young children and are more likely to be white. It has also been suggested that higher-income families tend to move very long or very short distances. This is presumably because their greater wealth makes the higher cost of moving a long distance worthwhile, and a shorter move costs relatively less for a richer than a poorer family.[3] Finally, and despite expectations, pensioner households are less likely to be influenced in their moves by quality of life factors. Although pensioners have less economic attachments to an area (through employment) it is likely that age and social connections reduce their overall ability and desire to move.[4]

Thus, it can be seen that there is a complex interaction between economic and social factors relating to migration, which is mediated by London's transport systems. Transport allows Londoners the freedom to move out of the capital while maintaining employment within it. In addition, it allows those living outside the capital to compete with London residents for jobs. Within London, transport also allows people to change jobs to other parts of London without necessarily needing to move house.

Age and lifestyle have also been identified as key mediating factors. Young single people flock to London for work and leisure activity, yet when they start families there is a tendency for them to leave the urban environment in search of an improved 'quality of life'. If they become very affluent they may return, but many expectations of retirement may not be fulfilled.

In this entire complex pattern it is probably during the ages of 25 to 50 that the labour market has the greatest part to play in migration. Job

---

[2] Higher Education Funding Council for England, *Regional Profiles of Higher Education* (2000).
[3] P H Rossi, *Why Families Move,* London (1980) p 24.
[4] A Rogers, ed., *Elderly Migration and Population Redistribution: a comparative study,* London (1992).

opportunities encourage recent graduates to stay in London rather than returning 'home'. Chapter 5 will identify the possession of a degree as the qualification at which competition between residents and commuters begins. These commuters include many young families who have left London for lifestyle reasons, as well as long-distance movers from outside the South East seeking jobs. The over-50s are less likely to move for either economic or quality of life reasons.

Migration, housing and commuting

However, added to these environmental pressures are housing market pressures, which in the United Kingdom are greatest in London. There is a net outflow of people each year from London to the rest of the South East created by people moving out because of the relatively higher priced housing in London. The National Housing Federation calculate that to buy an average property people will have to earn more than £30,000 in all but one of the London boroughs. Given that 70 per cent of households have incomes below £30,000, it is clear that there are large sections of the population that cannot afford housing in London and are being forced to live elsewhere. This is causing considerable concern about 'essential workers' – nurses, teachers and police officers, for example – who are often tied to a national pay scale, being driven out of London (leading to shortages of these workers in central areas) or facing long-distance commutes to get to work.[5]

This is exacerbated by the fact that the 'London effect' on house prices is spreading out of London into the rest of the South East. The most expensive boroughs outside London are South East districts, all of which figure largely in the commuting areas shown in Table 4.2. There have been a number of housing 'hotspots' reported for many years – Bath, Brighton, Oxford and Cambridge (all of which have attractive environments and are commutable to London) – but the spread of high-cost housing is now beginning to move out of Central London and into all parts of the South East.

There is thus conclusive evidence that the labour market for certain workers, particularly recent graduates in public sector occupations such as

---

[5] National Housing Federation, *London: a Tale of Two Cities*, London (2001) and *ibid, Mind the Gap: Housing London's Key Workers*, London (2001).

Table 4.3 House prices and required earnings in London boroughs

	Average house price	Household income required
Most expensive inside London	£	£
Kensington & Chelsea	567,962	179,851
Westminster	403,353	127,728
Camden	337,911	107,005
Hammersmith & Fulham	300,398	95,126
Richmond	287,366	90,999
Least expensive inside London		
Lewisham	131,485	41,637
Bexley	119,790	37,934
Waltham Forest	117,960	37,354
Newham	110,227	34,905
Barking & Dagenham	90,786	28,749
Most expensive outside London		
Windsor & Maidenhead	248,945	78,833
Surrey	222,318	70,401
Buckinghamshire	198,840	62,966
Wokingham	195,121	61,788
West Berkshire	173,256	54,846

Source: National Housing Federation
Note: Level of earnings required is calculated on the basis of a 95 per cent mortgage and 5 per cent deposit, based on the purchaser borrowing three times annual income

teaching and nursing, is affected by high house prices in London. In the last section we noted the tendency of young graduates to stay in London, rather than returning to their parents' homes in other regions of the United Kingdom. House prices are preventing such graduates from staying in London in these key occupations.

London also faces a number of difficulties in its housing. It has an older housing stock than the United Kingdom as a whole; 34 per cent of houses in London were built before 1919, compared to 25 per cent for the United Kingdom. At the same time, the rate of build of new houses in relation to the overall population of the city has been lower than that for the country as a whole. This index of change in the housing stock would need to be adjusted to take into account numbers of conversions, demolitions and vacancies before an overall change in the number of houses can be calculated.

In examining the degree to which this housing stock meets the needs of the population of London, account must be taken of changing social patterns including marriage, divorce and the overall size of families (including children and grandparents). There is an overall trend towards higher demand for smaller, particularly single person, housing. Major factors driving this include earlier ages for leaving parental home, fewer children, higher divorce rates, early retirement and longevity. This encompasses several different groups, including young people becoming independent from their families and pensioners maintaining an independent household after the death of one partner. It also includes an increase in childless couples, both independent pensioner households and younger couples. London has the lowest average household size of any region in the United Kingdom.

One of the contributing factors to this picture has been the development of commuting, which as we have seen has been associated with young families' migration out of London. Beginning in the 1930s, the construction of large suburbs has encouraged many who work in London to live further and further from the capital. The establishment of the London Green Belt in 1935 created a legally protected zone of substantially open land around London. It has led to a clear differentiation between 'Outer London' and the 'commuter districts' of the Home Counties that lie beyond it. This distinction may sometimes be one that is based more on perceived than real differences, as there are clearly 'urban' environments in many 'commuter' towns.

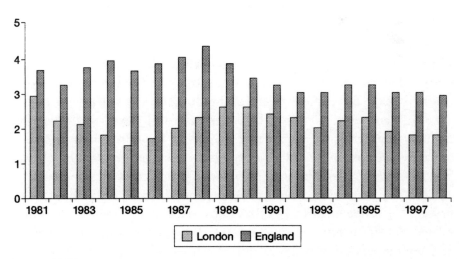

Source: DETR

Figure 4.2 Number of new house completions per '000 population, 1981–1998

The development of the M25 orbital motorway in the 1980s has also reinforced a division between those who live within it and the commuters who live beyond, even though in transport terms it may take less time to travel into London from outside the M25/Green Belt zone than to travel from Outer London to the centre.

The movement to live outside London has been driven by house-price differentials (in broad terms, the further from Central London, the cheaper the house costs) and by the attractions of a better environment (larger gardens, less traffic, better amenities). The increasing emphasis on a high-quality environment has encouraged pressure for new housing both on more distant communities outside London and on remaining open areas within the capital.

Thus, housing supply and availability have also influenced the patterns of migration and affected the labour market. High prices in London have prevented some groups from taking employment there and have encouraged the exodus of young families in search of a better quality of life. An older housing stock and lower level of new build make it more difficult for the housing market in London to respond to changes in demand.

Housing and regeneration areas

Naturally, not all housing in London is subject to market prices; some is 'affordable' housing owned by housing associations and some is public housing owned by local councils. The policy of council house sales begun in the early 1990s, particularly the so-called 'right to buy' for sitting tenants, has resulted in the loss of more attractive council housing stock. Councils have increasingly been left holding the stock that is in poorer condition and which tends to be concentrated in the poorer boroughs, discussed earlier as the regeneration areas of London. There has been much debate among specialists as to whether this has resulted in 'ghetto-isation', or the concentration of the poorest people in particular estates.[6]

This requires discussion on housing and social policy that is well beyond the scope of this work, but one aspect of this question is closely related to our current topic. There are many policy initiatives aimed at creating employment in these council estates. When people from these

---

[6] See, for example, the work of Professor Alan Murie of the University of Birmingham.

estates obtain stable employment, they often tend to move away to avoid the stigma attached to living in a poor estate. Such 'discrimination by post-code' can make it hard to obtain loans or jobs simply because a particular address is associated with poverty and deprivation.

The concentration of deprivation in particular areas of London is thus also a contributing factor to migration, as it leads families from such estates who are successful in obtaining employment to move to other parts of London, or indeed to move to cheaper housing beyond the capital. Moreover, other disadvantaged people such as refugees and other recent international migrants will often replace people who move from such poor estates, as the new arrivals will be drawn from council lists of those in need of housing. This movement of successful people out of poor estates to be replaced by more disadvantaged groups is one reason for the persistence of poverty for over 20 years in certain parts of London. Areas may have persistent high unemployment because as soon as residents obtain a job they move out.

Thus, added to the patterns of migration described earlier we must add a flow of disadvantaged into the regeneration areas of London, and a flow out from them of those that successfully move into and up the labour market. Barriers such as 'postcode discrimination' can limit these flows and serve to create an artificial brake on the workings of both the labour market and migration.

After completing this analysis of the constraints and choices that deter-mine the patterns of commuting and migration in London, we now turn to a comparison of the characteristics of commuters and residents, and the impact of travel on their working lives.

Time spent commuting

The downside for people living away from their work is that they must spend time commuting. As would be expected from the discussion above, the time that it takes to get to work in London is greater than anywhere else in the country, and it is increasing.

Data from the 1999 Labour Force Survey (Table 4.4) show that across Great Britain the average time taken to travel to work was 25 minutes, with 47 per cent of all workers taking less than 20 minutes, and 80 per cent less than 40 minutes. In London, the average time taken to travel to work was 42 minutes, with only 22 per cent taking less than 20 minutes to get to work and 51 per cent taking less than 40 minutes.

The situation was particularly severe in Central London, where average travel to work time was 56 minutes and lengthy commutes to work are common. Sixteen per cent of workers took more than 90 minutes to get to work, 49 per cent more than 60 minutes and 74 per cent more than 40 minutes.

The commuting patterns of people working in London are also very different to those of people in other areas. In the United Kingdom as a whole, 70 per cent of people usually travelled to work by car, with 11 per cent walking to work and 8 per cent going by bus. Six per cent used rail services and a minority 3 per cent cycled. Motorcycles were also in a minority at 1 per cent. Outside London, there is very little regional variation. In London, only 43 per cent commuted by car, a proportion that fell to 13 per cent in Central London. Of those working in Central London, 69 per cent travelled by train, with 31 per cent using the Underground and 38 per cent surface rail systems.

Patterns of travel to work also show marked differences between different groups of Londoners. For example, ethnic minorities are more likely than white people to look for jobs and be recruited by people of their own communities in their local borough. There are also significant differences in mode of travel. Almost half of all Asians tend to travel to work by car, more than for any other ethnic group including white people. Black people by contrast are more likely than other groups to go to work by bus. White people most commonly use the train – a reflection of commuting patterns.[7]

Table 4.4 Time taken to get to work

	Cumulative percentage				Mean time (minutes)
	<20 minutes	<40 minutes	<60 minutes	<90 minutes	
Great Britain	47	80	91	97	25
London	22	51	70	90	42
Central London	4	26	51	84	56
Rest of Inner London	22	51	70	91	42
Outer London	37	71	85	95	31

Source: Labour Force Survey, 1999

---

[7] See LSFU and Westminster Business School, *Strength Through Diversity* (1999), and LSFU, *Ethnic Capital* (2000).

Thus, the accessibility of different types of jobs to different groups of people is related to the availability of different kinds of transport with which to get to them. It is commonly assumed by those not from London that is very easy to move around the city, but in fact the ability to accept a job in one part of London very much depends on whether there is convenient and affordable means of transport to get to work.[8]

It is often noted that the speed of rush-hour traffic in London now is the same as it was over 100 years ago. This is used as an argument to demonstrate that public transport has not improved. It is important to remember, however, that the pattern of living and working was very different as related to the use of transport. One hundred years ago many of the least-skilled workers lived relatively close to where they worked and so walked to work, while levels of commuting and car use were minimal or non-existent. As a result, journeys were relatively short and opportunities to work outside the local area limited. If the comparison must be made (which is dubious given the completely different circumstances), the average worker would find it much easier to travel to work now than in the early 1900s.

Differences between commuters and residents

The arguments presented so far have presented many of the constraints that determine who becomes a commuter as opposed to living and working in London. It is necessary, however, to establish an overall picture of the 'typical' commuter and resident.

The traditional 'economic' view of commuters is that they incur additional costs and expenses to commute and therefore they must occupy higher paid jobs than non-commuters in order to justify that extra cost. It thus follows that commuters are more likely to have all the other characteristics of people who attract higher earnings – being more highly qualified, highly skilled and in higher-level occupations. This view needs questioning.

The impact of house prices in London is changing this traditional view in that it could be argued that high house prices are forcing people on lower salaries out of London. On this line of reasoning, the people who commute are the low paid (and again the corollary of lower average qualification levels, lower skills and lower-level occupation).

---

[8] CEBR, *Two Great Cities*, Corporation of London (1997) considers that the inefficiencies of London's transport system reduce the potential productivity of the capital in comparison to the Paris region.

A more subtle characterisation could include some commuters as having high-level occupations but low salaries. Public sector workers are tied to national salary scales which, even after allowing for London weighting allowances, are lower than the wages paid for equivalent jobs in the private sector. Public sector workers are less able to afford housing costs in London and are therefore faced with the choice of commuting in or moving out of London altogether. As the public sector also employs a high proportion of highly qualified people (many workers in the health service and education sectors require a degree of higher qualification in order to gain access to work), this would result in commuters who were more highly qualified, though not more highly paid.

A final subtle characterisation classifies commuters as those not able to enter the London housing market. This suggests that people who live in London can afford to do so because they already have a place in the housing market in London – often from parents or other relatives. Increasing house prices have no effect on them because their house value increases at the same time and at the same rate. If they decide to move, the incremental value of a more expensive house is less because they already own a house with its own inflated London price. Anyone seeking to move into London has to pay considerably more to purchase a house of the same standard as the one they already own outside the capital. In this sense, commuters are those people who do not have a place on the housing market. The main effect is to restrict the mobility of labour, preventing new workers moving house into London by increasing journey costs and travel times.

A number of these issues can be examined by comparing the characteristics of commuters and non-commuters, people who live and work in London. However, the results are generally not convincing in either direction. Looking first at an individual's personal characteristics, there are a number of distinct patterns:

- Men are slightly more likely to be commuters than women, reflecting the lower pay and caring duties that restrict women's ability to work.
- As people get older they are more likely to be commuters, which fits with the earlier suggestion that as people form relationships and start families they will move out of the city to find more spacious accommodation.
- People from white ethnic minority groups are more likely to be commuters than people from other ethnic groups. Ethnic minorities

are more likely to be discouraged from commuting by low pay and the need to maintain close links with their communities in London.
- People without disabilities are slightly more likely to be commuters than those with disabilities. This probably reflects access issues and caring responsibilities, in addition to low income.

The level of variation with each of these factors is relatively slight, however, and not clear-cut.

There is little variation in the level of qualification or skill held and the likelihood of being a commuter. Thirteen per cent of those with no qualifications commute, as do 14 per cent of those with a Level 5 qualification. The relationship between skills is more variable, but shows no consistent pattern. There is a slight tendency for the highly qualified or highly skilled to be more likely to commute,[9] but it would seem that high qualifications or skills, on their own, are not strongly associated with commuting.

Table 4.5 Variation in commuting status by personal characteristics

	Live in London	Live outside and commute	Base
	%	%	
Male	84	16	3,811
Female	87	13	2,957
Age			
16–24	88	12	1,271
25–30	89	11	1,446
31–40	85	16	1,912
41–50	85	15	1,187
51–60	79	21	673
61–64	89	11	62
Ethnicity			
White	85	15	5,720
Asian	89	11	473
Black	94	6	428
Mixed race	90	10	87
Other	93	7	57
Disability			
Disabled	88	12	269
Not disabled	86	14	6,477

Source: London Skills Survey, 2001

9   A similar relationship between qualifications and commuting – a slight tendency for the more highly qualified to be commuters – was observed in the London Skills Survey for 1997, 1998 and 1999.

Table 4.6 Variation in qualifications and skills by commuting status

	Live in London	Live outside and commute	Base
Qualification level	%	%	
No qualifications	87	13	912
Level 1	87	13	218
Level 2	87	13	1,523
Level 3	86	14	1,153
Level 4	85	15	2,379
Level 5	86	14	573
Composite skills needed score			
Very low	84	16	38
Low	88	12	281
Neither low nor high	87	13	1,744
High	87	13	3,399
Very high	82	18	1,305
Composite skills held score			
Very low	91	9	11
Low	86	14	175
Neither low nor high	86	14	1,587
High	88	12	3,134
Very high	83	17	1,860

Source: London Skills Survey, 2001

As can be seen from Table 4.7, managers and administrators are more likely to commute, thus supporting the hypothesis that higher-level occupations with consequently higher salaries are more likely to commute. This is also suggested by a lower level of commuting among plant and machine operatives, personal and protective occupations and 'other'. However, the pattern is not uniform as people in craft and related occupations are equally likely to commute as managers.

People who work in public services – education and health – are least likely to commute. This may suggest that although low-paid workers in these groups cannot afford London housing, they cannot afford to commute either. Alternatively, employment patterns may be more a reflection of skill shortages and hard-to-fill vacancies than of costs of commuting.

Overall, while there is some evidence that people with higher skill levels and in particular occupations are more likely to be commuters,

Table 4.7 Commuting rates among different occupational groups

	Live in London	Live outside and commute	Base
Occupational group	%	%	
Managers and administrators	80	20	1,463
Professionals	86	14	1,018
Associate professional and technical	89	11	1,057
Clerical and secretarial	88	12	1,026
Craft and related	80	20	480
Personal and protective	90	10	593
Sales	88	12	392
Plant and machine operatives	90	10	349
Other occupations	91	9	392
Industry sector			
Agriculture, mining and electricity, gas and water	80	20	59
Manufacturing	83	17	463
Construction	78	22	389
Wholesale and retail trade	85	15	954
Hotels and restaurants	87	13	336
Transport and communications	85	15	538
Financial intermediation	83	17	458
Real estate, renting and business services	84	16	1,149
Public administration	88	12	504
Education	90	10	613
Health and social work	91	9	745
Other community, social and personal activities	91	9	546

Source: London Skills Survey, 2001

there is not a great variation in these variables. The larger and more consistent variations in commuting emerged from the personal character-istics – gender, age and ethnicity – listed in Table 4.5. This supports the hypothesis presented during discussion of migration that it is mainly for lifestyle reasons that people who work in London decide to live outside the capital.

Conclusion

Approximately 14 per cent of people who work in London commute in from outside the city's boundaries. At a local (borough) level there is more commuting. On average, about 50 per cent of people live and work in the same borough.

Those who are commuting into London come, as would be expected, from the regions and counties that surround London. Surrey, Kent, Essex and Hertfordshire account for nearly three-quarters of all commuters. Long-distance commuting from further afield is a relatively rare phenomenon.

Being a 'commuter' is not a static position. The 'traditional' pattern is that as people grow older and their personal circumstances change (particularly forming a relationship and starting a family), people move out of London. This move often leads to a period of commuting, which can be protracted, until they can find a suitable job more local to their new home. The increase in relative house prices in London is having an impact on commuting patterns, forcing people to move out greater distances.

As a result, the time spent getting to work in London (and particularly Central London) is roughly twice that in all other areas in the United Kingdom. Nearly three-quarters of people who work in Central London take more than 40 minutes to get to work, with the average travel to work time being 56 minutes.

This chapter has demonstrated the existence of a complex series of economic relationships that determine where people live and work in London. The unemployed and people on low incomes are likely to live in areas of council housing which, as has been seen in Chapter 3, may not be within easy travelling distance of job opportunities, particularly when there is little money to spend on transport.

This chapter has mainly discussed the various constraints with regard to London as a whole, but it is important to point out that similar constraints on movement also exist at local level, where availability of transport and the character of local neighbourhoods can determine social relations, travel patterns and economic activity such as use of local shops.

When Londoners begin to start their own families, they tend to move out of London, in order to obtain cheaper housing and a better quality of life, which is often at the cost of a long and expensive journey to work. If highly successful, people may move further into the countryside or back into London, where a high salary may allow purchase of a more valuable property.

The higher levels of qualification, NVQ Level 3 and above, are where residents have to compete for jobs with those living outside London. It would seem that it is from this level of qualification upwards that the salary and prospects of jobs are such that people outside London become interested in them.

This chapter has also set out a number of dimensions of the complex relationship between where people live and where people work. Commuting and travel to work in London are thus intricately related to lifestyles, house prices and the high salaries in London that are needed to maintain them. It has been demonstrated that for someone already established in London and the South East, journey times and availability of transport have a great impact on the choice of employment. However, for someone with a job in London, lifestyle rather than economic issues are more likely to determine where they live. These constraints on how and where people move affect the labour market in a wide variety of ways, thus limiting the number of people who are interested in jobs in particular parts of London, while leaving jobs in much of Central London open to commuters from some distance outside the capital. Much of the operation of the labour market in practice happens through the transport and housing choices discussed in this chapter.

5

Qualifications, Skills and Learning of the London Workforce

As might be expected from its name, the London Skills Forecasting Unit (LSFU) has undertaken a wide range of research on skills issues and sees training as one of the most important issues facing London today. It should be no surprise, therefore, that this chapter is one of the longest in this book.

It is generally believed that a highly skilled workforce makes a company more competitive, and makes a region more supportive of business by creating a culture of innovation, continuous learning and a high level of technological development (see Chapter 3). This chapter explores the skills and qualifications of the London workforce, testing the assumptions in this belief.

Importance of qualifications and skills

The qualification and skill levels of London's workforce matter because London's employers need a workforce that has a range of skills and abilities to run their businesses effectively and to allow them to compete against others on a local, national and global scale. It can be argued that employers are most interested in the skills that allow them to compete and that qualifications *per se* are not important. However, it is generally recognised that while employers find it difficult to recognise skills, qualifications are easy to recognise and to verify. Employers use qualifications as a screening device, on the assumption that high skills and qualifications are to some extent correlated.

Qualifications matter to individuals, therefore, because they are a 'positional good'[1] in that they act as a screening mechanism by means of which good jobs are distributed. Following the initial entry into a job, the experience, training and vocationally related qualifications that accrue then act as further positional goods to gain access to better jobs. In short, good qualifications allow access into a positive cycle of high-level employment, learning opportunities and high salaries.

Throughout the 1980s, the lack of competence of the UK workforce became an increasingly important concern. Comparisons between the skill and educational capacity of our workforce with those of our principal competitors established that, broadly speaking, our workforce was worse educated and worse trained. This undermined our ability to compete effectively with them.

In response to these concerns, the National Training and Education Targets were launched in 1991 to set clear measurable goals in the educational attainment, skill levels and degree of participation in training of the British workforce. The 'National Targets' have recently been revised and a new date set for their attainment. The targets listed below are all to be achieved by 2002.

- Targets for 11 year olds
    - 80 per cent of 11 year olds reaching the expected standard for their age in literacy;
    - 75 per cent reaching the standard in numeracy.
- Targets for 16 year olds
    - 50 per cent of 16 year olds gaining 5 higher grade (A-C) GCSEs;
    - 95 per cent gaining at least one GCSE.
- Targets for young people
    - 85 per cent of 19 year olds having a Level 2 qualification;
    - 60 per cent of 21 year olds having a Level 3 qualification.
- Targets for adults
    - 50 per cent of adults having a Level 3 qualification;
    - 28 per cent of adults having a Level 4 qualification;

---

[1]   Discussed in F Hirsch, *The Social Limits to Growth*, London (1977) and E Keep and K Mayhew, *What makes training pay*, Institute of Personnel and Development (1998).

- – a 7 per cent reduction in the 26 per cent of adults who have not participated in learning.
- Targets for organisations
  - – 45 per cent of medium-sized organisations recognised as Investors in People;
  - – 10,000 small organisations recognised as Investors in People.

The Learning and Skills Council was established in April 2001. It brings work-based learning and vocational training under one administration. It is considering new national and local targets for 2002–2010, which will continue the drive towards increased participation, lifelong learning and increased national competitiveness.

The remainder of this chapter concentrates on the qualification and skill levels of the current workforce – those covered in the targets for adults in the 'Target' definitions used above.

As can be seen from above, the Targets are all set in a context of 'levels'. This is because the range of qualifications that people can obtain varies widely. They include academic qualifications that can be gained from school, college or university, and vocational qualifications that tend to be more work-based and are gained while in employment. There are also many qualifications that contain an element of both: people who have a job are often studying simultaneously for qualifications at a college. Some higher-level qualifications are purely vocational, although they are often not described as such – professions such as doctors, nurses, engineers and accountants have qualifications which are purely related to a job, often gained in universities while the individual is not working. To simplify this wide range of qualifications, a comparative framework called the NVQ Level Framework was introduced. It places all qualifications against a 'level' starting at Level 1, the lowest, through to Level 5.

Table 5.1 shows how different qualifications fit into this framework, but in general terms a degree counts as Level 4, two A level passes as Level 3, 5 GCSEs as Level 2. Some qualifications have their own levels: National Vocational Qualifications (NVQs) are awarded at different levels and other vocational qualifications such as RSA and City and Guilds are awarded at 'Higher', 'Advanced' or 'Basic', which all are placed at different levels in the NVQ Level Framework.

How London works

Table 5.1 Common qualifications and the NVQ Level Framework

Qualification	NVQ Framework level
Degree-level qualification, higher degree or equivalent	Level 4 and above
Diploma in higher education	Level 4 and above
Degree-level professional qualifications	Level 4 and above
HNC/HND	Level 4
ONC/OND	Level 3
BTEC, BEC or TEC	Higher = Level 4
	Nationals = Level 3
	Firsts = Level 2
SCOTVEC, SCOTEC or SCOTBEC	Higher = Level 4
	Nationals = Level 3
	Firsts = Level 2
Teaching qualification	Level 4
Nursing or other medical qualification	Level 4
A Level	2 passes or more = Level 3
	1 pass or less = Level 2
AS Levels	4 passes or more = Level 3
	1 pass or less = Level 2
Scottish Certificate of Education	Higher = Level 3
	Standard/Ordinary = Level 2
NVQ/SVQs	NVQ level 4 = Level 4
	NVQ level 3 = Level 3
	NVQ level 2 = Level 2
GNVQs	Advanced = Level 3
	Intermediate = Level 2
	Foundation = Level 1
O Levels, GCSEs, CSEs	Five passes or more = Level 2
	Four passes or less = Level 1
RSA	Higher = Level 4
	Advanced = Level 3
	Basic = Level 2
Pitmans	Advanced = Level 3
	Intermediate, other = Level 2
City and Guilds	Advanced = Level 3
	Craft = Level 2
	Other = Level 1
YT Certificate	Level 1

Overall qualification levels

The NVQ Level Framework allows us to have an overview of qualification levels that is easy to understand. Looking at Table 5.2 we can see that, overall, people who work in London have a high level of qualifications. Thirty-six per cent are qualified to Level 4 and above, with another 18 per cent qualified to Level 3. However, just less than one-quarter have no or very low levels of qualifications, with 18 per cent having none and 5 per cent qualified only to Level 1.

It is useful to see London in context of the rest of the United Kingdom, using data from a national data set, the Labour Force Survey (LFS).[2] It is clear from this that people who live in London are, on average, qualified to a higher level than elsewhere in the United Kingdom. We can see that:

- There are 10.7 million economically active adults qualified to at least NVQ Level 3, equivalent to 46 per cent of the adults in England. London has 1.8 million people qualified to at least Level 3, some 52 per cent of the relevant population. This is the highest rate of all the Government Office regions.
- There are 6.2 million adults qualified to at least NVQ Level 4, which is 26.5 per cent of economically active adults in England. London has 1.2 million people qualified to at least Level 4, an attainment rate of 35 per cent. Again, this is the highest rate of all the Government Office regions.

Table 5.2 Overall level of qualifications in London

Qualification level	%
No qualifications	18
Level 1	5
Level 2	24
Level 3	18
Level 4	29
Level 5	7
Total	*100*

Source: London Skills Survey, 2001

---

[2] The LFS is the only central source of data that can measure adult attainment that is comparable across the whole of the United Kingdom. The results are not directly comparable to those produced by the London Skills Survey and the percentages qualified at different levels will vary.

Table 5.3 Qualifications of the workforce, London and England compared, 1999

	NVQ Level 3		NVQ Level 4	
	Total number	*Proportion of adult population*	*Total number*	*Proportion of adult population*
(n = thousands)	n	%	n	%
England	10,762	46.0	6,213	26.5
London	1,807	52	1,221	35
East of England	1,142	44	635	24
East Midlands	849	42	462	23
North East	468	42	236	21
North West	1,424	46	773	25
South East	1,961	50	1,177	30
South West	1,064	46	612	26
West Midlands	1,029	41	566	23
Yorkshire & the Humber	1,018	44	531	23

Source: LFS, based on data provided by the DfEE for the Government Office for London

In respect of the National Targets, as London has a higher 'baseline' attainment rate of people who are qualified (ie the starting position when the Targets were announced), it is of no particular surprise that the Government Office for London has been set higher targets than other regions and England as a whole. While the national Target has been set at 50 per cent of adults to be qualified at Level 3 and 28 per cent at Level 4 by 2002, the London target has been set at 56 per cent for the Level 3 Target and 37.4 per cent for the Level 4 Target.

Overall skill levels

As noted earlier, employers are not only interested in qualifications, but are perhaps more interested in the skills that the qualifications represent. However, while qualifications are readily identified and measured, skill levels (particularly the wider generic skills) are much more difficult to answer consistently. While some can be measured and have qualifications attached (basic skills such as reading and writing, IT skills), many others have no certification and are much harder to identify. While there is some linkage between the level of occupation, qualification, skill and pay, none of these can be used as a reliable measure of how well somebody can carry out a task at work.

As a result of the lack of certification, there is also the problem of definition. This concerns both actual definition of what is meant by a skill and the level of skill. What one person may mean by 'communication' may not concur with another. Communication may be understood by some as talking face to face, by others as including talking on the telephone, by others as writing notes or messages to people and by others as the ability to use e-mail. In some definitions, the use of e-mail may be included in the use of IT. With regard to levels, there are problems defining competency: for one person the ability to read may require the person to read Shakespeare, while in some jobs it may equate to simple instructions such as 'this way up' on a box.

Research[3] has indicated that there is some considerable confusion among employers over these skills. When employers are asked about what they mean by various skills, the results show that there are many skills for which the component parts show a good deal of overlap. Different employers appear to use different terms for what is essentially the same skill. Thus, for example, the component parts of 'oral communication', 'interpersonal' and 'customer service' skills are essentially the same, with a focus on the ability to talk and listen to other people, whether they be customers/clients or other members of staff or colleagues. Similarly, the elements of 'time management' and 'organisational' skills are the same, with an emphasis on an individual's ability to take responsibility for their own workload.

To address these problems, two approaches to the definition and measurement of skills are in the early stages of development. On definition, the term 'generic skills' has been coined to distinguish a set of general skills that are transferable across different jobs. These skills are considered to be different from vocational or job-specific skills that are not transferable between jobs. The list of key generic skills normally includes:

- basic communication;
- numeracy;
- IT;
- ability to work with others (often referred to as team working);

[3] M Spilsbury and K Lane, *Skill Needs and Recruitment Practices in Central London*, Focus Central London (2000).

- problem solving;
- reasoning skills for work planning;
- work process management skills;
- ability to improve one's own learning and performance.

In addition to 'generic skills', there is also a definition of 'soft' skills, which include team leadership, negotiation, facilitation and social skills (the ability to get on with others). However, this list of skills is by no means definitive and there is some debate over its content.

Skills measurement

There have been three broad approaches to measuring skills related to specific occupations and jobs. These are:

- using professional job analysts to identify precisely what skills are needed to carry out their jobs;
- asking employees precisely what skills they need to carry out their existing job and then whether they think that they have those skills. This has a problem of objectivity – people tend to list the skills they have, rather than all the skills that the jobs need. As a result, the range of skills required by jobs is often understated;
- asking employers what they think the skills are. Again, this has problems in that employers may not realise the full extent of the skills being used in the jobs, and may well under-value the role of generic skills.

The London Skills Survey used the second of these approaches – namely, asking people what skills were needed to do their jobs (or a job that they would like to do) – and then asked them whether they had these skills. The individuals were asked about eight 'skill elements' that may have been part of their current job, or part of a job that they may want to do in the future. They were also asked to rank these on a scale running from 'not at all important' to 'essential'.[4] They were then asked about how

---

[4]   The entire scale is 'not at all important' (which has been awarded a value of 1), ' not very important' (2), 'fairly important' (3), 'very important' (4) and 'essential' (5). These numeric values have been used to create mean scores in which the higher the score, the more important the skill is in doing the job.

Table 5.4 Job-related generic skills in the London Skills Survey

Skill	Task element
Communication skills	Communicate with others by being able to deal with and listen to customers and colleagues
Team working	Work in a team by being able to work with and help others in your team
Initiative	Show initiative, by acting without being prompted and being relied on to get the work done
Literacy skills	Write or read notes, instructions, forms, manuals or reports
Problem solving	Be able to solve problems by spotting problems or faults and then being able to think of a solution
Numeracy skills	Have number skills by being able to carry out calculation, using a computer or calculator if necessary
Management skills	Have management skills by planning the activities of others or by leading a team
IT skills	Use a computer, PC or other type of computerised equipment.

Table 5.5 Overall level of skills needed for jobs in London

Qualification level	Communi- cation skills	Team working	Initiative	Literacy skills	Problem solving	Numeracy skills	Management skills	IT skills
	%	%	%	%	%	%	%	%
Not at all important	0	1	1	1	1	1	3	9
Not very important	3	4	4	4	5	9	16	12
Fairly important	18	21	23	21	24	29	32	24
Very important	39	43	42	48	47	41	30	33
Essential	38	29	28	24	21	18	18	20
Mean score (n)	*4.13*	*3.99*	*3.95*	*3.90*	*3.86*	*3.66*	*3.44*	*3.43*

Source: London Skills Survey, 2001

Table 5.6 Overall level of skills held in London

How often done effectively	Communi- cation skills	Team working	Initiative	Literacy skills	Problem solving	Numeracy skills	Management skills	IT skills
	%	%	%	%	%	%	%	%
Hardly ever	0	0	0	0	0	0	2	7
Sometimes	3	3	4	2	3	7	15	10
Often	20	22	23	18	25	27	28	25
Nearly always	37	39	38	45	46	43	31	34
Always	40	35	34	34	26	23	22	23
Mean score (n)	*4.14*	*4.06*	*4.01*	*4.12*	*3.94*	*3.81*	*3.56*	*3.57*

Source: London Skills Survey, 2001

effectively they could do these tasks.[5] The task elements that were covered and the associated 'skill' are shown in Table 5.4.

The most important skill across all jobs is the ability to communicate – the ability to deal with and listen to customers and colleagues. Thirty-eight per cent of people think this essential and 39 per cent think it very important. No people believed that it was not at all important for their job. The next most important skills are team working and showing initiative.

The skill that is held at the highest level is literacy skill, with nearly eight out of ten people believing that they are effective in this domain. After this, the ranking of skills held more or less mirrors the ranking of skills needed.

IT skills

When asked about skills problems in these areas of generic skills, employers in the 1998–2000 annual London Employer Surveys have always reported IT to be their biggest problem. Despite this, individuals have reported in the annual London Skills Surveys from 1998–2000 that IT is the generic skill that is the least important for their jobs.

The skill that is regarded as least important overall is IT. This may initially seem surprising, given the emphasis afforded to this skill area, but it is important to note that while IT skills are regarded as being essential by 20 per cent and very important by 33 per cent of people, relatively high proportions of people do not regard them as an important skill, with 9 per cent saying that they are not important at all, and a further 12 per cent saying that they are not very important. The responses for management skills are similar, with about one-fifth saying that this skill is not at all, or not very, important. Essentially, the low ranking given to IT and management skills is because there are a number of jobs for which these skills are simply not relevant.

The only skills that are not thought to be held to any great extent are IT skills (where 7 per cent say that they can hardly ever deliver these skills effectively and 10 per cent say that they can only effectively deliver these

---

[5]   In this case the scale runs from 'hardly ever able to do this effectively' (value of 1), 'sometimes do this effectively' (2), 'often able to do this effectively' (3), 'nearly always do this effectively' (4) and 'always do this effectively' (5). Again, mean scores have been calculated and a high average score indicates a high skill level.

skills sometimes) and management skills (2 and 15 per cent respectively). There is no doubt a correlation between the need to have these skills in a job, as seen above, and the extent to which people hold them. If people do not actually need to have these skills in their job, they do not develop them.

However, when individuals are asked about their training preferences, IT skills are their most popular choice. Over one-fifth of those employed in 1998 and 1999 report having no IT skills. In 1999, over one-third of the unemployed also reported that they had no IT skills, thus raising the prospect of a 'digital divide' between those with and those without the ability to use IT in a job or to look for employment and training.[6]

Employers thus place more emphasis on IT skills than employees do. Nevertheless, employees are very interested in training on this topic, which is likely to be a key one for the competitiveness of London's economy.

Qualifications and skill level

Because qualifications and skills act as access routes into different jobs, it is important to see who has these qualifications and skills and who has not.

There is a clear relationship between the level of qualification that a person holds and the level of skills that a person holds. This is the case across all the skills, as shown in Table 5.7. People at each level of qualification hold the same profile of skill levels, ie literacy and communication skills are held to the highest levels and IT skills and management skills to the lowest. Equally, the highly qualified are more likely to hold each skill to a higher level. The lowest level of IT skills (the skill held least of all the skills) is held by those with no qualifications. At the other end of the scale, the highest level of communication skills is held by those with the highest level of qualification.

There is thus, as one would expect, a close relationship between level of skill and level of qualification. This demonstrates that employers are right to use qualifications as a proxy for skill level.

---

6   LSFU, *Creating the Learning Capital* (2001).

Table 5.7 Level of qualifications and level of skills in London (mean scores)

Qualification level	No qualifications	Level 1	Level 2	Level 3	Level 4 and above
Communication skills	3.68	3.83	4.05	4.17	4.46
Team working	3.59	3.76	3.94	4.09	4.50
Initiative	3.59	3.66	3.88	4.04	4.35
Literacy skills	3.65	3.86	4.02	4.17	4.43
Problem solving	3.50	3.66	3.81	3.97	4.26
Numeracy skills	3.32	3.46	3.69	3.88	4.16
Management skills	3.03	3.04	3.36	3.56	4.02
IT skills	2.75	3.06	3.39	3.72	4.08

Source: London Skills Survey, 2001

Personal characteristics

The level of qualification does not vary by gender to any great degree: women are only slightly less likely to have no qualifications and slightly less likely to be qualified to higher levels. There are clearer relationships between the age of people and the qualifications they hold. Older people, particularly those over 51, are more likely to have no qualifications. Younger people (those aged 16–24) are less likely to have higher-level qualifications (Level 4 and above), but this is more due to the fact that a

Table 5.8 Overall level of qualifications in London

Qualification level	No qualifications	Level 1	Level 2	Level 3	Level 4	Level 5
	%	%	%	%	%	%
All	18	5	24	18	29	7
Men	17	4	23	18	30	8
Women	19	5	26	17	28	6
16–24	17	8	32	29	14	1
25–30	15	3	20	17	38	8
31–40	16	4	24	14	33	9
41–50	19	3	22	12	34	10
51–60	30	3	20	11	29	7
61–64	36	4	17	9	30	5

Source: London Skills Survey, 2001

high proportion of these (ie all those aged under 20) will still be in the process of gaining their higher-level qualifications.

There is little difference between the levels of ability in the various skills between men and women. The only skill areas where there is some, albeit slight, difference are the areas of IT and management skills, where men rate themselves as having slightly higher levels of skills.

The youngest and oldest age groups tend to rate themselves as having the lowest levels of skill, with the level of skill peaking somewhere in the middle age group, most frequently in the 41–50 age group. This accords well with the profile of qualifications. IT skills are highest among the 25–30 age group, beyond which they decline quickly.

Table 5.10 shows different qualification levels by different ethnic groups, showing both broad (in bold) and detailed groupings. It is useful to show this because it gives a good indication of how grouping data can actually conceal differences within overall groups.

At a broad level, there is relatively little difference between qualification attainment levels of ethnic groups. The proportion of whites, Asians, Blacks and those of mixed race with no qualifications are roughly the same (being between 16 and 19 per cent), with only the 'Other' group having a higher proportion. The proportion of whites with higher-level qualifications (Levels 4 and 5) is higher, at 37 per cent, compared to around 30 per cent for the other three main groups.

However, when we look at the more detailed classifications we see a wider variety. Among the white group, it is clear that there is a high proportion of Irish and 'Other' groups with no qualifications. Among

Table 5.9 Level of skills held, age and gender in London (mean scores)

	Communi-cation skills	Team working	Initiative	Literacy skills	Problem solving	Numeracy skills	Management skills	IT skills
All	4.14	4.06	4.01	4.12	3.94	3.81	3.56	3.57
Men	4.15	4.08	4.03	4.11	3.95	3.85	3.61	3.63
Women	4.14	4.04	3.99	4.13	3.92	3.78	3.50	3.50
16–24	4.06	3.93	3.88	4.02	3.78	3.70	3.27	3.55
25–30	4.21	4.14	4.06	4.17	4.01	3.88	3.62	3.71
31–40	4.14	4.08	4.05	4.15	3.98	3.83	3.63	3.59
41–50	4.23	4.14	4.11	4.20	4.02	3.89	3.72	3.53
51–60	4.11	4.06	4.04	4.08	3.94	3.77	3.69	3.35
61–64	3.94	3.81	3.78	3.88	3.80	3.68	3.54	2.73

Source: London Skills Survey, 2001

How London works

Asians, we can see that 'Other Asians' are nearly twice as likely as the other Asian groups to have no qualifications.

The evidence on skills shows that people who belong to Black groups assess their skill ability as the lowest, with the others being roughly equal. Low skills are less likely to be found among sub-groups such as the Irish or the Bangladeshi communities than low levels of qualification. This may be one of the instances where the correlation between skills and qualifications is weaker.

The London Skills Survey has produced a consistent picture of ethnic groups in the capital over the period 1997–2001. Black African and Indian groups have similar levels of qualification to white groups, but qualification rates for Bangladeshis and Black Caribbean groups are significantly lower. However, all ethnic minority groups have at least double the rate of unemployment of the white population. Policy towards African and Indian groups should therefore concentrate on improving employment

Table 5.10 Overall level of qualifications in London

Qualification level	No qualifications	Level 1	Level 2	Level 3	Level 4	Level 5
	%					
All	**18**	**5**	**24**	**18**	**29**	**7**
White	**18**	**4**	**25**	**17**	**30**	**7**
British	15	5	26	17	30	7
Irish	31	1	25	16	21	6
Other	38	3	9	18	26	6
Mixed	**17**	**3**	**31**	**19**	**20**	**9**
White & black	19	5	30	13	25	8
White & Asian	30	0	18	18	20	14
Other	5	3	41	32	11	8
Asian/Asian British	**19**	**4**	**22**	**24**	**25**	**7**
Indian	13	5	21	27	28	5
Pakistani	19	3	23	23	27	5
Bangladeshi	12	5	30	25	16	12
Other	34	4	16	17	20	9
Black/Black British	**16**	**8**	**27**	**20**	**24**	**6**
Caribbean	15	10	33	18	18	5
African	20	5	18	22	29	6
Other	4	10	28	21	35	3
Other	**36**	**5**	**18**	**14**	**22**	**5**
Chinese	30	6	14	19	23	9
Other	38	5	20	12	22	3

Source: London Skills Survey, 2001

120

prospects, whereas policy for Black Caribbean and Bangladeshi groups should concentrate on improving educational attainment.[7]

Finally, looking at disability, people who classify themselves as having a disability or long-term illness are twice as likely not to have any qualifications. Similarly, people who do not have a disability are more likely to believe that they possess each of the skills to a higher average level than people who have a disability.

The London Skills Survey has provided evidence for the need to improve the supply of learning to the disabled, their ability to access learning, as well as the need to change the attitudes of both the disabled and training providers.[8]

Table 5.11 Level of qualifications and disability in London

Qualification level	Has disability	Does not have disability
	%	%
No qualifications	34	17
Level 1	5	5
Level 2	20	25
Level 3	13	18
Level 4	22	29
Level 5	6	7
Total	*100*	*100*

Source: London Skills Survey, 2001

Qualifications and work

There is a clear link in London between having a qualification and being in work. As can be seen in Table 5.12, over a third (34 per cent) of the unemployed have no qualification, as do just over a quarter (27 per cent) of the inactive.[9] People who are in work are much more likely to have higher level qualifications – 44 per cent of the employed are qualified to Level 4 and above, compared to 18 per cent of the unemployed and 14 per cent of the inactive.

---

[7] LSFU, *Strength through Diversity* (1999) and *Ethnic Capital* (2000).
[8] LSFU, *Creating the Learning Capital* (2001).
[9] The distinction between the unemployed and inactive is that the unemployed are those who are actively seeking work, the inactive are people who have not looked for work in the last four weeks.

Table 5.12 Level of qualifications and economic status in London

Qualification level	All	Employed	Unemployed	Inactive
	%	%	%	%
No qualifications	18	14	34	27
Level 1	5	3	9	7
Level 2	24	23	27	30
Level 3	18	17	13	22
Level 4	29	35	14	12
Level 5	7	9	4	2
Total	*100*	*100*	*100*	*100*

Source: London Skills Survey, 2001

The skill levels of the employed are also uniformly higher than the skills held by the unemployed and the inactive. There is little difference between the level of skills held by the unemployed and inactive.

The employed have a higher estimation of the skills required in work, and the inactive have a higher estimation than the unemployed (Table 5.13). This could be because the unemployed do not have job experiences which allow them to correctly assess the levels of skill needed. It could also be because the jobs held by the employed (who have, on average, higher-level qualifications) include a measure of higher-level occupations to which many unemployed would not have access. These higher-level occupations require higher levels of skills and therefore the skills required by the employed as a whole are higher than the levels of skills required by the unemployed in order to obtain a job.

Thus, it is clear that qualifications are correlated with economic status, with people in work being more likely to have higher-level qualifications and vice versa. The relationship is reinforced by a strong link between qualification level and occupation. For a few occupations, such as in the medical profession, a formal qualification is a necessity to practise. However, for many others, those carrying out a job can often possess a broad range of qualifications.

The data show that the people who work in professional occupations are the most highly qualified, with 90 per cent qualified to Level 4 and above. Essentially, a degree or higher-level qualification is a necessity to work in these jobs. Fifty-nine per cent of managers and senior officials also have a higher-level qualification, as do 62 per cent of those in associate professional and technical occupations.

Table 5.13 Level of skills and economic status in London (mean scores)

	All	Employed	Unemployed	Inactive
Skills required in job				
Communication skills	4.13	4.21	3.83	3.97
Team working	3.99	4.06	3.74	3.83
Initiative	3.95	4.04	3.64	3.72
Literacy skills	3.90	3.98	3.54	3.77
Problem solving	3.86	3.94	3.49	3.67
Numeracy skills	3.66	3.72	3.32	3.55
Management skills	3.44	3.57	2.98	3.15
IT skills	3.43	3.47	3.02	3.44
Skills possessed				
Communication skills	4.14	4.25	3.82	3.88
Team working	4.06	4.18	3.74	3.75
Initiative	4.01	4.13	3.70	3.73
Literacy skills	4.12	4.21	3.82	3.89
Problem solving	3.94	4.05	3.58	3.68
Numeracy skills	3.81	3.93	3.43	3.54
Management skills	3.56	3.73	2.99	3.14
IT skills	3.57	3.72	3.01	3.22

Source: London Skills Survey, 2001

Table 5.14 Qualification levels and occupation in London

Qualification level	No qualifications	Level 1	Level 2	Level 3	Level 4	Level 5
	%	%	%	%	%	%
All employed	14	3	23	17	35	9
Managers and senior officials	7	2	15	17	46	13
Professional occupations	3	0	3	5	65	25
Associate professional & technical occupations	6	1	14	18	54	8
Clerical and secretarial occupations	11	4	31	27	24	2
Skilled trade occupations	19	4	42	22	12	1
Leisure and other personal service occupations	23	4	34	23	15	1
Sales and customer service occupations	20	7	35	29	9	1
Process, plant and machinery operatives	36	2	47	8	6	0
Elementary occupations	37	12	34	12	5	0

Source: London Skills Survey, 2001

Table 5.15 Level of skills held, age and gender in London (mean scores)

	Communi-cation skills	Team working	Initiative	Literacy skills	Problem solving	Numeracy skills	Management skills	IT skills
Skills required in job								
Managers and senior officials	4.45	4.33	4.36	4.27	4.18	4.06	4.19	3.88
Professional occupations	4.54	4.40	4.38	4.41	4.32	4.13	3.98	4.09
Associate professional and technical occupations	4.46	4.30	4.30	4.25	4.20	3.80	3.75	3.77
Clerical and secretarial occupations	4.21	4.03	3.98	4.15	3.89	3.86	3.38	3.85
Skilled trade occupations	3.77	3.69	3.68	3.46	3.70	3.34	3.17	2.66
Leisure and other personal service occupations	4.09	3.86	3.91	3.66	3.88	3.35	3.38	2.77
Sales and customer service occupations	4.07	3.80	3.72	3.64	3.58	3.61	3.10	2.97
Process, plant and machinery operatives	3.52	3.29	3.40	3.29	3.41	3.00	2.83	2.55
Elementary occupations	3.52	3.48	3.31	3.05	3.19	3.01	2.71	2.26
Skills possessed								
Managers and senior officials	4.46	4.43	4.42	4.44	4.28	4.20	4.24	4.07
Professional occupations	4.57	4.51	4.45	4.54	4.38	4.28	4.12	4.24
Associate professional and technical occupations	4.50	4.43	4.36	4.44	4.27	4.12	3.94	4.00
Clerical and secretarial occupations	4.28	4.17	4.11	4.27	4.05	3.97	3.58	3.92
Skilled trade occupations	3.89	3.85	3.76	3.86	3.72	3.59	3.35	3.02
Leisure and other personal service occupations	4.08	3.98	3.95	4.02	3.87	3.60	3.48	3.21
Sales and customer service occupations	4.08	3.96	3.88	4.01	3.80	3.78	3.38	3.44
Process, plant and machinery operatives	3.56	3.45	3.49	3.55	3.49	3.23	3.04	2.71
Elementary occupations	3.65	3.56	3.51	3.58	`3.43	3.31	2.95	2.87

Source: London Skills Survey, 2001

Below this, there is more of a mix of qualification level. In some occupations, roughly equal numbers of people have different level qualifications. In clerical and secretarial occupations, for example, 31 per cent have a Level 2 qualification, 27 per cent a Level 3 and 26 per cent a Level 4 and above. Jobs at the lower end of the occupational spectrum, particularly elementary occupations, are more likely to be carried out by people with no or very low levels of qualifications.

The skills required in the job also vary by occupation. In general terms, the higher the level of occupation, the higher the level of skills needed. Thus, managers and senior officials and professional occupations have the highest skill requirements; process and plant and machinery operatives and elementary occupations have the lowest.

Table 5.15 also demonstrates that people naturally believe that they possess a higher level of skill than is required to do their job.

The data do not prove that qualifications are necessary to obtain a job. Indeed, many employers say that they are not. Nevertheless, the fact that employed people are not likely to possess skills and qualifications, and people in higher occupations are most likely to possess skills and qualifications, suggests that *de facto* a certain level of qualification is necessary.

Lifelong learning

In recent years, there has been a distinctive change in the approach to the continuing development of the workforce. It has generally been accepted that there is a need to make a reality of lifelong learning: the increasing pace of change means that those who continuously improve their knowledge and skills throughout their lives have the best chance of remaining employable and adapting to rapidly changing economic circumstances. If people do not upgrade their skills, the consequences can be damaging. There is a widening wage gap between high-skilled and low-wage workers. Many people are trapped by a lack of education, leading to a poorer chance of finding secure and satisfactory work. Lifelong learning is needed so that:

- people who have failed at school are not condemned to a lifetime at the lower reaches or the margins of the workforce;
- people's skills do not erode over time;
- employers have a source of skilled labour to ensure the responsiveness of industry to the increasingly competitive economy.

The drive to expand the extent of learning is a major part of the drive to tackle social exclusion. In the United Kingdom in August 2001 there were still more than 1.5 million unemployed (using the ILO definition), of whom over one-quarter were long-term unemployed (unemployed for more than 12 months).[10] A large number of the working-age population now appears to form a workless class who have become cut off from the world of work and who appear to be fatalistic about their prospects. There is a growing body of policy that seeks to address this section of the population, most particularly the New Deal for young and long-term unemployed people. However, to be consistent, the Targets also need to address the needs of these people.

To reflect the increased emphasis on social inclusivity, there is now a Learning Participation Target included as part of the National Targets. This is the first time that a Target has been set which aims to include a measure of the extent to which people in this country are engaged in learning. It will be unlike the other Targets in that this one is a participation target, while the others are all couched in terms of achievements or outputs in the form of qualifications. This new Target is an important indicator of how well the United Kingdom is progressing towards becoming a more learning-focused society.

At a national level, the baseline for adult participation in learning was measured by the National Adult Learning Survey (NALS), undertaken for the first time in 1997. The definition that the NALS uses for 'participation in learning' is wide. A person is classified as a 'learner' if they have undertaken any of the following activities during the last three years:

- **taught learning**
  - any taught classes that were meant to lead to qualifications;
  - any taught courses designed to help develop skills that might be used in a job;
  - any courses, instruction or tuition in driving, playing a musical instrument, in an art or craft, in a sport or in any practical skill;
  - evening classes;
  - learning which has involved working on one's own from a package of materials provided by an employer, college, commercial organisation or other training provider;
  - any other taught course, instruction or tuition.

---

[10] Data from Labour Market Trends, Office for National Statistics, August 2001. The actual numbers of unemployed are 1,661,000, of whom 449,000 have been unemployed for more than 12 months. The level of unemployment using the claimant count measurement is 939,000, of which 193,000 (21 per cent) have been unemployed for more than 12 months.

- **non-taught learning**
  - studying for qualifications without taking part in a taught course;
  - supervised training while actually doing a job (ie when a manager or experienced colleague has spent time with an employee helping learn or develop skills as specific tasks are done at work);
  - time spent keeping up to date with developments in the type of work done without taking part in a taught course – eg by reading books, manuals or journals or attending seminars;
  - deliberately trying to improve knowledge about anything or teaching oneself a skill without taking part in a taught course.

It was found that 26 per cent of the adult population had not participated in learning in the previous three years,[11] even with the fairly broad definition of learning used in NALS. The existence of a hard core of 'non-learners' who have not participated in learning in the recent past and who have no intention of participating in the future is well documented. As the NALS research has shown, those who are less likely to be learners are the excluded – those with few or no qualifications, in low-skilled jobs, in unemployment or out of the labour force. Given that the definition of 'learning' was wide and the time span was over the previous three years, this group could be described as 'dedicated' non-learners.

The London Skills Survey also asks individuals about their involvement in taught and non-taught learning and when they were last involved in such learning. From this, we have constructed a four-way schema that describes learning behaviour. This split is shown below for the last three years (a period which equates to the definition used in the National Targets) and the last 12 months, so that we can examine 'recent' learning patterns.

These data show that in the last three years, the majority of Londoners (90 per cent) have undertaken some learning, with only 10 per cent stating that they have done neither taught nor non-taught learning. Looking more recently, 78 per cent have undertaken learning in the last 12 months.

These results suggest that the extent of learning is considerably higher in London than the average across the country – we will return to discuss why this should be the case later.

---

[11] P Beinart and P Smith, *National Adult Learning Survey, 1997*, DfEE Research Report 49 (1998).

Table 5.16 Learning behaviour in London

	Last 12 months	Last 3 years
	%	%
Taught learning only	4	4
Non-taught learning only	29	15
Both taught and non-taught learning	45	70
No learning	22	10

Source: London Skills Survey, 2001

Variation in learning patterns

The NALS research found that the groups that were particularly unlikely to have taken part in learning in the past three years included:

- those aged 50 or over;
- those looking after the home or family;
- the retired and those unable to work because of long-term sickness;
- those who had left school aged 16 or younger without qualifications.

People who were more likely to have taken part in learning were males, younger people, those in paid work, those working in managerial, professional or other non-manual occupations, those who stayed in full-time education longer, and those who left it with better qualifications.

These linkages between personal characteristics and learning behaviour are confirmed by the data from the London Skills Survey, but these data also confirm a number of other points. There is a correlation between the likelihood of having undertaken learning and an individual having qualifications and skills. Those with higher-level qualifications and higher-level skills were more likely to have undertaken learning in the last 12 months than those with lower qualifications and lower skills. Nearly nine out of ten of those qualified to degree level and above (Level 4) had undertaken learning in the last 12 months, while 39 per cent of those with no qualifications had undertaken no learning.

Table 5.17 shows a skills index which aggregates and then averages all the individual skill components into a single score. This demonstrates quite clearly the relationship between skills and the likelihood of learning. Sixty-two per cent of those with the lowest skills had not undertaken any learning in the last 12 months, while 83 per cent of those with the highest skills had done so.

Following on from this link between learning, qualifications and skills, the relationships that have been seen earlier of being in work and the occupational status of that work also apply to learning. However, it is likely that the direction of causality is different. While higher levels of qualification and skills usually obtained in formal education before the age of 25 may lead to a higher chance of being employed and employed in a higher level of occupation, the chances of receiving learning are increased if an individual is in work and in a high-level occupation after formal education has ended. In short, the majority of learning that is undertaken beyond formal schooling is done in a work-based environment.

It can be seen in Table 5.18 that the majority of taught learning experiences (54 per cent) address skills that might be used in a job.

The majority of taught learning experiences are related to the individual's current job or a job that they may want to do, and indicate the strength of the link between work and learning. Relatively few learning activities have been undertaken for the individual's own personal interest or development. Among the unemployed and inactive, learning activities

Table 5.17 Learning in the last 12 months, qualifications and skills in London

	Taught learning only	Non-taught learning only	Both taught and non-taught learning	No learning
	%	%	%	%
All	4	29	45	22
Qualifications				
No qualifications	3	33	26	39
Level 1	6	29	35	30
Level 2	5	28	42	25
Level 3	3	27	55	15
Level 4 & above	5	29	53	14
Skills held				
Very low skills	0	27	10	62
Low skills	3	35	14	49
Medium skills	2	35	39	24
High skills	3	27	50	20
Very high skills	9	25	48	17

Source: London Skills Survey, 2001

Table 5.18 Learning in the last 12 months in London, qualifications and skills

Type of learning	
(multiple response)	%
Taught learning	
Taught classes that were meant to lead to qualifications	42
Taught courses designed to help develop skills that might be used in a job	54
Courses, instruction or tuition in driving, playing a musical instrument, in an art or craft, in a sport or in any practical skill	3
Evening classes	1
Learning which has involved working on one's own from a package of materials provided by an employer, college, commercial organisation or other training provider	4
Any other taught course, instruction or tuition	5

Source: London Skills Survey, 2001

that have been undertaken tend to relate to work, but in this case to work that will be wanted in the future. Although learning for one's own personal interest and development is more important for people in the unemployed and inactive groups, it is still a minority of the learning experiences.

Finally, to emphasise the importance of work in learning, it is clear that in the majority of cases where there were costs, these costs were borne by the employer. Overall, 53 per cent of the costs of taught learning were borne by employers.

Again, there are considerable variations by working status – learning activities that have no costs involved are more important for the unemployed and inactive.

Thus, most post-formal education learning activity occurs in work and is

Table 5.19 Reason for taught learning activity in London

	All	Economic status		
		Working	*Unemployed*	*Inactive*
Multiple response	%	%	%	%
Related to current or previous job	60	79	24	6
Related to a job that might be wanted in the future	37	22	71	80
Own personal interest or development	24	17	34	43

Source: London Skills Survey, 2001

Table 5.20 Who paid for the taught learning activity in London

	All	Economic status		
		Working	*Unemployed*	*Inactive*
	%	%	%	%
Employer	53	69	18	3
Trainee	21	18	26	30
Both	1	1	0	*
Someone else	8	3	26	21
No costs involved	18	9	29	45

Source: London Skills Survey, 2001

supported by the employer. This learning is most likely to be strengthened by influencing the employer, the individual, and by increasing provision for those not in work.

Comparing London and the UK learning rates

As discussed briefly above, the rate of learning participation in London is higher than that found in the NALS research for the United Kingdom overall. It is worth briefly considering the extent of the comparability of the NALS research and the London Skills Survey. The survey approaches and the questions used in both surveys are broadly comparable, although there will inevitably be differences introduced by different sampling strategies etc. As has been seen, the propensity to learn varies with the likelihood of being in work, qualification level, skill level and occupation. As London has a workforce which is more likely to be in work, more likely to have higher-level qualifications (and therefore skills, although we do not have a measurement for this) and more likely to be in higher-level occupations, the fact that people who work in London are more likely to have undertaken some learning should not come as a great surprise.

Change in qualifications and skills over time

There is no doubt that overall qualification levels of the workforce are increasing over time. Table 5.21 shows the change in proportion of those who are qualified to Level 3 and to Level 4 in London and the rest of the United Kingdom.

- At Level 3, London has shown a steady increase over the four years, increasing from 47 per cent in 1996 to 52 per cent in 1999. Over the same period, the proportion qualified in England overall has also increased steadily at a similar rate, from 41.4 per cent in 1996 to 46 per cent in 1999;
- At Level 4, the proportion qualified in London has also shown a steady increase over the four years, increasing from 32 per cent in 1996 to 35 per cent in 1999. England overall has also shown a steady increase over each of the four years, increasing from 23.9 per cent in 1996 to 26.5 per cent in 1999.

However, this is not a recent phenomenon – the demand for qualified people has been rising rapidly since the 1970s. This increased demand for well-qualified people has been the result of two main changes:

- changing patterns within occupations, whereby the proportions qualified at higher levels within occupational groups have increased;
- shifts in the occupational structure, which has led to increases in those groups that employ larger proportions of highly qualified people.

The first change can be demonstrated by showing, in Table 5.22, the growth in the proportion of the employed workforce who are qualified at degree levels in 1981, 1991 and 1998. There have been general increases in

Table 5.21 Adults qualified to Level 3 and Level 4

	Level 3				Level 4			
	1996	*1997*	*1998*	*1999*	*1996*	*1997*	*1998*	*1999*
	%	%	%	%	%	%	%	%
England	41.4	42.8	44.5	46.0	23.9	24.4	25.7	26.5
London	47	49	50	52	32	33	34	35
East of England	40	40	42	44	22	21	23	24
East Midlands	39	40	42	42	22	21	22	23
North East	40	38	41	42	21	19	21	21
North West	40	42	44	46	22	23	24	25
South East	44	46	48	50	26	27	29	30
South West	41	44	45	46	24	25	26	26
West Midlands	37	39	40	41	21	21	22	23
Yorkshire & the Humber	39	41	42	44	21	22	23	23

Source: DfEE and Government Office for London

the proportion of people holding these jobs in most of the 'higher-level' occupations. There have been particular increases in some areas – for example, in 1981 just over one in ten (13 per cent) of corporate administrators had higher-level qualifications, and by 1998 this had increased to just less than one in three (31 per cent). However, this should not

Table 5.22 Graduate penetration by occupation 1981–1998 (percentage qualified at degree level or above)

	Percentage of men and women with a first or higher degree		
	1981 %	*1991* %	*1998* %
Managers and senior officials			
Corporate administrators	13	20	31
Managers and proprietors	3	6	8
Professional occupations			
Science and engineering professionals	43	46	51
Health professionals	96	96	97
Teaching professionals	60	66	78
Other professionals	61	63	72
Associate professional and technical occupations			
Science associate professionals	16	20	25
Health associate professionals	3	5	12
Other associate professionals	17	22	27
Clerical and secretarial occupations			
Clerical occupations	2	4	6
Secretarial occupations	2	2	3
Skilled trade occupations			
Skilled construction trades	0	1	1
Skilled engineering trades	1	1	1
Other skilled trades	0	1	1
Leisure and other personal service occupations			
Protective service occupations	2	2	5
Personal service occupations	1	1	2
Sales and customer service occupations			
Buyers, brokers and sales representatives	5	8	11
Other sales occupations	1	1	2
Process, plant and machinery operatives			
Industrial plant and machinery operatives	1	1	1
Drivers and mobile machinery operatives	0	0	1
Elementary occupations			
Other operatives in agriculture	1	1	2
Other elementary occupations	0	1	2

Source: Projections of occupations and qualifications 1999–2000, Institute for Employment Research, 2000

disguise the fact that there are large swathes of jobs that are, by and large, 'graduate-free' and which show no signs of taking on graduates in any large numbers.

Table 5.22 focuses on higher-level qualifications, but there have also been changes below this level; there have, for example, been large increases especially at Level 3, particularly in clerical and secretarial, protective and personal service and sales occupations.

In addition, over the period 1981–1998, the total number of people employed increased from just under 25.5 million to just over 27 million. Within this overall pattern there have been significant shifts, with those occupations that have relatively lower levels of qualification declining both in actual and relative terms. The number of jobs in elementary occupations has declined by 650,000, which has seen its relative share of all employment decrease from 18 per cent to 14 per cent. At the other end of the scale, the number of people employed in professional occupations has increased by nearly one million, increasing the occupational share from 8 per cent to 11 per cent.

At the same time, the total supply of graduates has risen equally rapidly, driven by increasing proportions of young people staying on in full-time education and gaining formal qualifications. This tendency, which has accelerated further in the past decade, is the result of a number of factors, including rising incomes, easier access, changing social class structure and

Table 5.23 Occupational employment, 1981–1998

	Employment levels					
	1981		*1991*		*1998*	
	'000	*%*	*'000*	*%*	*'000*	*%*
Managers and senior officials	2,530	10	3,281	13	3,620	13
Professional occupations	1,968	8	2,410	9	2,936	11
Associate professional and technical occupations	2,301	9	2,870	11	3,350	12
Clerical and secretarial occupations	3,833	16	4,083	16	4,047	15
Skilled trade occupations	4,256	17	4,026	16	3,738	14
Leisure and other personal service occupations	859	4	1,205	5	1,525	6
Sales and customer service occupations	1,452	6	1,660	6	1,801	7
Process, plant and machinery operatives	2,967	12	2,589	10	2,455	9
Elementary occupations	4,321	18	3,891	15	3,671	14
Total	*24,488*	*100*	*26,014*	*100*	*27,143*	*100*

Source: Projections of occupations and qualifications 1999–2000, Institute for Employment Research, 2000

changes in the examination system (there was, for example, an increase in the staying on rate after the introduction of GCSEs). Pressures on educational institutions to increase student numbers have reinforced all these factors.

These trends among young people have been reinforced by a growing tendency for older people to go back into formal education at later stages in their lives.

This analysis suggests that levels of skills and qualifications have been driven by both employer demand and educational supply. Many of the changes in occupation have in turn been driven by the economic changes set out in Chapter 1. The overall result has been that a higher level of skills and qualification than ever before is required to obtain a given job. At the same time, those without skills and qualifications have found themselves at an increasing disadvantage in the labour market. Lack of access to, or attainment in, education and training is thus becoming an increasingly critical factor in the labour market.

Looking to the future

The main trends have been forecast for the next decade. Assuming that there is a continuation of longer-term historical trends in the United Kingdom, there will be over two million additional jobs for highly qualified people (Levels 4 and 5) by the year 2009, compared with the level in 1998. Moreover, this is based on extrapolating observed trends from the 1980s and 1990s – if the experiences of only the 1990s are continued, demand could rise even faster than this.

London, which is already one of the most highly qualified areas in the United Kingdom, is set to increase at a faster rate than this. Again looking at projections for the future, in Table 5.25 we can see that to 2009 the number of overall jobs in the economy will increase by 11 per cent, but the number of highly qualified jobs will increase by 29 per cent. In London, the number of jobs will increase by 12 per cent, but the number of highly qualified jobs will increase by 40 per cent. As a result, therefore, demand for higher-level qualifications in London is set to increase.

The supply of highly qualified people is also set to continue very rapidly. The increase in educational participation rates which has already occurred in the 1980s and 1990s is expected to lead to an increase in the

Table 5.24 Occupational employment, 1998–2009

	Employment levels					
	1998		2004		2009	
	'000	%	'000	%	'000	%
Managers and senior officials	3,620	13	3,758	13	3,912	13
Professional occupations	2,936	11	33,72	12	3,803	13
Associate professional and technical occupations	3,350	12	3,748	13	4,169	14
Clerical and secretarial occupations	4,047	15	4,029	14	4,017	14
Skilled trade occupations	3,738	14	3,547	13	3,473	12
Leisure and other personal service occupations	1,525	6	1,786	6	1,993	7
Sales and customer service occupations	1,801	7	1,906	7	1,988	7
Process, plant and machinery operatives	2,455	9	2,384	9	2,421	8
Elementary occupations	3,671	14	3,606	13	3,613	12
Total	27,143	100	28,137	100	29,388	100

Source: Projections of occupations and qualifications 1999–2000, Institute for Employment Research, 2000

Table 5.25 Changing demand for skills and employment

	United Kingdom			London		
('000s)	1998	2009	% change 1998–2009	1998	2009	% change 1998–2009
All employment	26,548	29,389	11	3,895	4,351	12
Higher-level qualified jobs (NVQ Level 4 and above)	5,549	7,180	29	1,025	1,430	40

Source: Projections of occupations and qualifications 1999–2000, Institute for Employment Research, 2000

economically active stock in the United Kingdom of those qualified at higher levels (ie with a degree or higher) of 1.9 million in the United Kingdom by 2009 (when compared to 1998 levels). First-degree-level qualifications will account for around three-quarters of this growth. Naturally, if educational participation rates continue to rise (as many expect), the increase will be even greater.

One might argue that with the potential for a global economic downturn these arguments no longer apply, but this would be a mistake. An overall fall in employment will not affect – and indeed might even encourage – employers' demands for higher qualifications so that they can increase productivity.

Changing nature of skills

There is a frequent debate about the change in skill levels in society. There are three general schools of thought:

- up-skilling: that changes in the work place make even greater demands on the skills and understanding of the workforce, shifting their role from one of undertaking physical tasks to one of exercising judgement and control through a more profound understanding of the work being undertaken;
- deskilling: that jobs are becoming more simple as technology increasingly embodies the skills and discretion that were previously embedded in people;
- polarisation: which takes elements of both of the above arguments and argues that some jobs are being deskilled while others are requiring an increasing skill content.

This issue was explored in a national study of work skills.[12] The study found that the level of skills needed has increased between 1997 and 2001. There is almost no evidence of deskilling taking place and little evidence of polarisation. Of the people who had stayed in the same jobs, skills had risen in all occupations, some more than others, but there is no special tendency for lower-level occupations to have had below average level increases in skill requirements. There were differences between full- and part-time jobs, which suggest that the gulf between these may be widening, but this was not differentiated on an occupational basis. Some skills have become more important than others – in particular, computing skills have become more important, rising most for high-level occupations but also widely across the workforce at middling levels of sophistication. A good corroborating indicator is that having computer skills is associated with a substantial pay premium (even after controlling for other factors that impact on pay). It would seem that demand for computing skills has increased across the decade.

Research[13] has indicated that many employers have a weak demand for skills as a result of:

---

[12] D Ashton, B Davies, A Felsted and F Green, *Work Skills in Britain 2000*, SKOPE (2000).
[13] E Keep and K Mayhew, *Training Policy for Competitiveness: time for a fresh perspective*, Paper to the Skills Focus Conference (1994).

- shifts in the employment structure, which suggest that the economy is not moving to a uniformly-high skilled workforce. Rather there is a division appearing between high-skilled managerial and low-skilled workers;
- a higher proportion of workers shifting into the periphery – those with part-time work, on fixed-term contracts etc. Many of these peripheral jobs are likely to be lower skilled and of lower status and are less likely to receive training even though they still represent a minority of overall employment;
- a dwindling commitment to the domestic economy as mobile capital creates skilled jobs overseas. Some major British firms now have domestic operations that are a shrinking (and increasingly marginal) part of their overall businesses, which must raise doubts about their willingness to invest in training;
- low-level product market and production strategies, which accept low productivity in return for low wages.

This is not to say, of course, that there are not some companies which adopt a high-skill-level strategy, and of course it is perfectly feasible that the United Kingdom can have high- and low-skill sectors in co-existence. The balance between high-level and low-level employers is not clear, but it is evident that for some employers their chosen route to business success will not involve investment in their employees and nor will it involve the employment of highly qualified (and expensive) workers.

This viewpoint has led to some concern as it could be damaging in the long term – once an employer has embarked on a low-skill route their subsequent choice of working methods and technology will reflect and confirm that choice. This argument of a 'low-skill equilibrium' is one that is becoming increasingly popular. What is not clear, however, is whether the initial impetus to move to this position is due to poor quality supply of skills or a lack of demand from employers.

Thus, we are left with the position that while the Targets suggest that the majority of new entrants to the labour market will be qualified to Level 3 and half of the existing workforce will also be qualified to this level, it is not clear that employers actually want employees who are as well qualified as this. It is certainly the case that labour market entrants with Level 2 qualifications and below do find work. Will this change in the same time frame as the Targets? The evidence[14] suggests that employers are increasingly ensuring that their employees have the skills that they require:

- The proportion of employers providing off-the-job training for their staff has grown since the early 1990s.
- The United Kingdom is the leader in Europe in the volume of general management, technical and operational training carried out in small and medium-sized enterprises.

Whether or not this training equates to the qualification levels suggested in the Targets is a matter for some debate.

Intermediate skills problem

The debate about whether the United Kingdom has a worse educated workforce than our competitors is fairly contentious. Lower rates of education participation among 17 and 18 year olds are countered with statistics regarding the United Kingdom's higher rate of participation among mature students and lower educational dropout rate. There is less debate with regard to intermediate skills. A programme of work[15] has argued that the United Kingdom's deficiency lies mainly in the area of intermediate, vocational skills, with two main areas of weakness:

- In the United Kingdom, foremen or 'charge hand' workers are appointed for their managerial skills. The German equivalent is primarily a technical person who in addition has acquired further experience and the necessary managerial skills. As a result, the German level of technical competence is far ahead of the UK equivalent.
- The broad system to produce craft workers in Germany and elsewhere has produced a sound base for workers to master new skills required of them by new technology. In the United Kingdom, the number of crafts and apprenticeships has fallen steadily.

---

[14] NACETT, *Fast Forward for Skills* (1998).
[15] Conducted at the National Institute for Economic and Social Research.

As a result, the United Kingdom suffers from a shortfall in the number of craftsmen and technicians qualified to an intermediate level.

The argument which runs counter to this is that although the proportion who have qualifications at intermediate levels may be below that of our immediate competitors, this is by no means the same as saying that the proportion of our workforce who hold intermediate skills is less, as skills and qualifications are not the same thing. While it is certainly the case that there are many people in the workforce with either low-level or no qualifications, we cannot be sure that these are people without skills – rather, their skills do not equate to existing qualifications. NACETT believes[16] that there are indications that a significant number of people in the workforce have Level 3 skills but no qualification to attest to these skills. There is a need for research to identify whether actual qualification levels do underestimate the true stock of skills in the workforce and, if they do, to what extent.

Longer-term issues

As has been seen, by 2008 the number of people who hold higher-level qualifications is expected to increase by 1.9 million across the United Kingdom, about the same as the number demanded by employers. A simplistic calculation would therefore suggest that most people with higher-level qualifications would easily find jobs. However, it is unlikely to be that simplistic.

'Traditional' areas of graduate employment may find it difficult to cope with the large influx of newly qualified entrants expected in the next decade. While the jobs being created are for highly qualified people, many of them will also require levels of previous experience, often requiring sector-specific skills. In this scenario, the new entrants to the labour market will have to find new areas for employment as compared to previous generations. This did happen to an extent in the 1990s. Most newly qualified graduate-level people did find permanent employment, but there is evidence to suggest that the nature of many of the jobs is changing and the 'traditional' view of what is, and what is not, a graduate job is changing in two ways:

---

[16] NACETT, *Fast Forward for Skills* (1998).

- Many jobs are becoming more complicated, needing relatively greater knowledge and abilities.
- Better-qualified people are being employed in jobs previously carried out by those who were less well qualified.

Naturally, these two factors may well interact. Using better-qualified people may alter the way in which jobs are done and improve competitiveness. The supply of people with high-level qualifications may have led to an increase in demand for people with high-level qualifications, thus changing the nature of the job done. However, there are also possible downsides:

- Less well-qualified people may be displaced into less demanding jobs, more marginal jobs or unemployment.
- People who have just qualified at a higher level may find themselves in jobs that do not match their expectations, thus leading to a lack of job satisfaction.

Conclusion

Qualifications and skills are different but work closely together. Qualifications may be described as the 'coinage' of the labour market – a known value that enables employers and employees to establish a common value. Skills are then the 'fuel' of the labour market – skills, and particularly high skills, drive forward growth in productivity and innovation.

The link between qualifications, skills and employment has been shown to be a very complex association. The overall level of qualifications and skills in the workforce has risen, and this can be linked to the broader pattern of change in the economy described in Chapter 1. The situation with regard to demand for skills and qualifications from employers is more ambiguous. It would seem that the higher the occupation (more responsibility, more skill), the more employers have demanded high-level skills and qualifications. However, for some lower-level occupations there is less evidence of the need for higher skills and qualifications. Where employers feel that employees need skills, they provide training, although this may not be aligned with national qualification systems.

The evidence is also, however, that the unemployed, to whom we turn in Chapter 6, tend to have lower qualifications and receive less training, while those in work and highly qualified continue to gain more skills. Thus, it remains the case that further training is likely to enhance both employability and career advancement.

6

Unemployment

Unemployment, particularly over the long term, is a tragedy for both individuals and families. It is always hard to talk about such personal events in terms of generalities and statistics. Yet, if we are to understand the broader economic and social forces that lead to unemployment, we are in a better position to fight against it and to prepare to face the difficulties that all economies, and a great many individuals, inevitably face sometime in their lives.

The goal that unites every public sector and community agency in London is to reduce unemployment and poverty. There may be a variety of different understandings of both unemployment and poverty. There is a wide variety of roles which agencies assume to help achieve this goal; from improving housing conditions, reducing the cost of transport to work, job creation, job subsidy, training, encouraging inward investment etc. The central problem of unacceptably high unemployment remains at the heart of the London economy, limiting the potential of the city to generate prosperity for all its citizens.

In 2001, London and the United Kingdom were enjoying their lowest unemployment rates for over 20 years (Table 6.1) and yet two London boroughs still had almost 10 per cent of their workforce as registered unemployed (Haringey and Lewisham, August 2001 claimant count).

Millions of pounds have been spent trying to reduce unemployment in London and yet it is still unacceptably high. Why is this? This chapter cannot provide an answer to a problem that so many agencies have been combating with so many different schemes for so long, but it will show why the problem is so persistent. The relatively high level of unemployment in 2001, at the end of a long period of successful growth in the capital, demonstrates in itself that the problem is not simply a case of the

Table 6.1 Unemployment trends in London and the United Kingdom, 1989–2001

	ILO unemployment rates		Claimant count rates	
	London	*United Kingdom*	*London*	*United Kingdom*
1989	6.8	7.2	5.3	6.6
1990	6.8	6.8	4.7	5.6
1991	9.1	8.4	7.5	7.6
1992	12.0	9.7	10.1	9.5
1993	13.2	10.3	11.7	10.5
1994	13.1	9.6	11.0	9.7
1995	11.5	8.6	9.6	8.2
1996	11.3	8.2	8.9	7.6
1997	9.1	7.1	6.9	5.9
1998	8.1	6.1	5.5	4.8
1999	7.5	6.0	4.9	4.6
2000	7.1	5.6	3.9	3.8
2001	6.0	4.9	3.3	3.3

Source: Office for National Statistics
Note: Unadjusted averages for Spring (March to May) quarters of each year based on those aged 16 or over

state of the economy. In fact, if unemployment in 2001 is still unacceptably high, it poses the question – what will happen when the economy next begins a cyclical downturn?

A non-technical note on measuring unemployment

Many people are now well aware that governments over the past 20 years have changed the way in which unemployment is calculated, and before looking at too many figures it is worth commenting on this point. An understanding of some of the broad principles behind the different measures is fundamental to an appreciation of how the figures reflect the status of being unemployed.

Table 6.1 shows the average unemployment rate in London and the United Kingdom during the spring quarter of each year from 1989 to 2001 by the two main measures of unemployment – International Labour Organisation (ILO) and claimant count. For those who are interested, the Office for National Statistics and appropriate government departments can provide technical detail on how they have made adjustments to allow trends in unemployment to be re-established under the latest measure.

The claimant count is a count of the number of those registered to receive unemployment benefit as a percentage of the resident workforce (those who are economically active – see below). The ILO measure, which is used as a standard throughout Europe, is based on the Labour Force Survey (LFS). The survey asks respondents who say they are unemployed whether they have been available for work and actively looking for a job during the preceding four weeks.

Thus, the claimant count shows the proportion of the workforce who are receiving benefit, whereas the ILO measure shows the proportion of the workforce who are looking for work. The ILO rate is always higher than the claimant count as many people who are actually looking for work are not eligible to claim benefit. Some, for example, are held to be not available for work because of other commitments – caring duties, voluntary work etc.

In 1989, the ILO rate for both London and the United Kingdom was within 1 per cent of the claimant count. In 2001, this gap had increased slightly in the case of the United Kingdom, but in the case of London the ILO rate is almost double that of the claimant count. This suggests that in 2001 a much larger proportion of those looking for work in London were not eligible for unemployment benefit than in 1989, and in 2001 people looking for work in London were less likely to be claiming benefit than in the rest of the United Kingdom. This gap has been growing for many years and is one reason why the government, in 1997, decided to adopt the ILO measure, as its official definition of unemployment. A large number of reasons might be suggested for this change: the growth of an informal economy (debatably larger in London than other parts of the United Kingdom); changes in eligibility for benefit; and growth in those classified as long-term sick and in carers for them; among others.

This brief discussion illustrates that both measures are important and should be used in appropriate circumstances. The ILO definition measures what most people would think of as unemployment: people who are looking for work. The Labour Force Survey in which this measure is collected also adds other useful information, such as the numbers of people who are in part-time work but who would actually like a full-time job, and much of this extra information will be used throughout this chapter. The claimant count shows the degree to which any area has a large number of people dependent on unemployment benefit. This measure can become important if we are trying to assess more precisely who is dependent on the State because they do not have a job.

Until 1997, the claimant count was used as the principal official measure of unemployment, but since then the ILO definition has been preferred.

Long-term change in unemployment in London[1]

Until 1992, unemployment in London was lower than that of the country as a whole (Table 6.2). In 1983, unemployment in London was 20 percentage points below that of Great Britain. This difference fell slowly until the 1990s when London's labour market experienced rapid decline and the regional unemployment rate fell below that of the country as a whole. During the early 1990s, the rate of unemployment in London rose to about 20 per cent above the national rate, but since 1995, as the economy has improved, London's position relative to Great Britain has slowly improved. These trends suggest that London tends to respond faster to adverse conditions in the national economy, and to recover more slowly when the national economy starts to improve.

London is linked to the South East by a number of economic links. In terms of the business environment, many larger companies have branches in both regions. Many London companies have suppliers and customers in South East England. Many of the higher-level employees in London companies live in the South East and commute to the capital. Londoners must compete with residents of South East England for jobs in the capital.

It is thus not surprising to note that the unemployment rate for London has a similar relationship to that in South East England as it does to that of Great Britain as a whole. In times of recession, the unemployment rate in London rises faster than it does in the rest of the South East (Table 6.2, Figure 6.1). When the economy improves, the unemployment rate for London falls more slowly than that of South East England (excluding London). Commuters tend to be the more highly qualified workers who can afford transport costs, and who have established a higher quality of life in a more suburban or rural environment. These workers may be less

---

[1]   This section owes much to unpublished work conducted by Hilary Metcalfe and Bernard Casey at the Policy Studies Institute in 1997, as well as to ideas developed by Ian Gordon.

likely to lose their jobs during a recession, leading to a higher differential rise in unemployment among London's lower-qualified residents. Equally, when job opportunities improve, the more limited availability of qualified London residents, and their need to compete with potential commuters from the South East (and indeed across the United Kingdom), means that unemployment in London falls more slowly.

Table 6.2 shows that during the 1980s the unemployment rate in South East England rose only briefly in 1985–1986 in relation to that of Great Britain as a whole, in contrast to London where unemployment rose earlier, in 1984, and did not fall before the next recession in the 1990s. Unemployment in the South East reached another high point in relation to Great Britain in 1992, but has fallen ever since, whereas in London the situation continued to grow worse and was only reversed in 1998. London did not have enough time to recover from recession in the 1980s before the 1990s' recession hit an already depressed labour market.

Figure 6.3 indicates that while the unemployment rate in London has improved in relation to that of Great Britain since 1997, it has not improved in relation to that of South East England. Indeed, London has seen a continuously deteriorating position relative to the South East on both the ILO (Figure 6.2) and claimant count (Figure 6.3) measures.

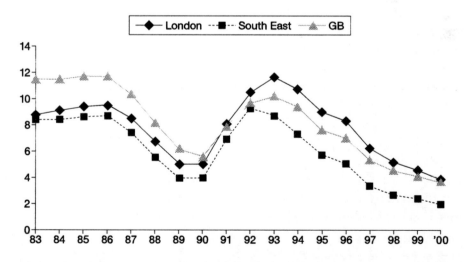

Figure 6.1 Unemployment rates (claimant count)

Table 6.2 Annual average claimant unemployment rate 1983-2000

	1983	1984	1985	1986	1987	1988	1989	1990	1991	1992	1993	1994	1995	1996	1997	1998	1999	2000
London	8.8	9.1	9.4	9.5	8.5	6.7	5.0	5.0	8.1	10.5	11.6	10.7	9.0	8.3	6.2	5.1	4.5	3.8
South East	8.4	8.4	8.6	8.7	7.4	5.5	3.9	3.9	6.9	9.3	8.7	7.3	5.7	5.0	3.3	2.6	2.3	1.9
GB	11.5	11.5	11.7	11.7	10.4	8.2	6.1	5.6	7.9	9.7	10.2	9.4	7.6	7.0	5.3	4.5	4.1	3.6
Ratio of unemployment rates																		
London/SE	1.05	1.08	1.09	1.09	1.15	1.22	1.28	1.28	1.17	1.13	1.33	1.47	1.58	1.67	1.88	1.96	1.96	2.0
London/GB	0.77	0.79	0.80	0.81	0.82	0.82	0.82	0.89	1.03	1.08	1.14	1.14	1.19	1.19	1.19	1.15	1.10	1.06
SE/GB	0.73	0.73	0.74	0.74	0.71	0.67	0.64	0.70	0.87	0.96	0.85	0.78	0.75	0.71	0.62	0.58	0.56	0.53
(London/SE)/GB	9.1	9.4	9.3	9.3	11.1	14.9	21.0	22.9	14.8	11.6	13.0	15.6	20.7	23.9	35.5	43.6	43.6	55.6

Note: breaks in the series occurred in 1986, 1988

Source: Employment Gazette/Labour Market Trends, January 1987; January 1991; July 1994; April 1997; June 1999; May 2001.

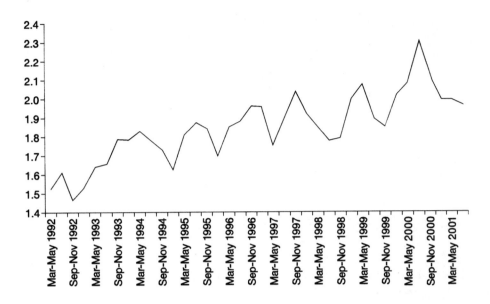

Figure 6.2 ILO unemployment rate in London/South East

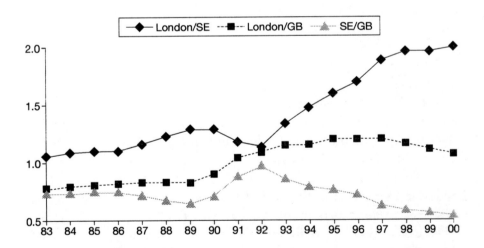

Figure 6.3 Relative unemployment rates (claimant count)

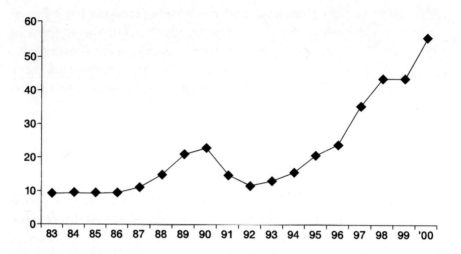

Figure 6.4 London to South East unemployment standardised by GB unemployment (London/ROSE)/GB*100

London's rapid response to deteriorating circumstances and its slower response to an improved economy means that London has most to gain from an economic cycle that leaves as long as possible between downturns. The longer that the economic outlook is positive, the more likely it is that London will be able to catch up with the South East. As soon as the economic situation worsens, London's tendency to rapid decline will mean that unemployment in the capital will quickly lose any relative improvement.

Ian Gordon has suggested[2] that unemployment only begins to fall significantly in London when the unemployment in South East England falls below 3 per cent. It is only when unemployment in the South East reaches this level that South East residents cease to compete with Londoners by commuting to jobs in the capital. For unemployment in London to match that in South East England, it would take between six and sixteen more years of uninterrupted growth.

These long-term cycles indicate the degree to which high unemployment in London is influenced by major strategic forces in the national and regional economies. It is more fragile than the adjacent South East region or the United Kingdom as a whole. Growth would appear to create fewer

---

2   In the *London – New York Study*, Corporation of London (2000), pp 18–19.

jobs in London than elsewhere, and conversely recession has a bigger impact in London than elsewhere. The trends illustrate the strength of forces with which those seeking to reduce unemployment must engage. London's level of unemployment has fallen throughout 2001 and, more than any other region, London has a strong interest in supporting continued growth in the national economy.

Seasonal patterns in unemployment

The previous section has identified the characteristic way in which London reacts to the national economic cycle of growth and recession, which is strongly linked to that of South East England. There is also a persistent seasonal cycle related to South East England that can be observed over almost 10 years (Figure 6.2).

Unemployment has a strong seasonal character. It tends to fall in the spring as seasonal jobs are created and the new financial year begins. It tends to rise in the autumn and winter as new school and college leavers have entered the market over the summer, and seasonal jobs and occupations (eg construction) slow for the winter. Figure 6.2 indicates that there is also a strong seasonal relationship between unemployment in London and South East England. London's unemployment rate falls more strongly than that of the South East during the spring, but this relative fall is more than countered by a very strong rise in unemployment during the autumn. It is not easy to come up with a simple explanation for this trend. It may be suggested initially that the greater spring fall in unemployment may be boosted by large numbers of London students returning home, or by intensive construction activity. However, in the autumn such seasonal work is more likely to cease in London than in the South East, leading to a relative rise in unemployment.

Long-term unemployment

Many people may experience some unemployment during their working lives, but unemployment is often of very short duration as people move between jobs. However, some people become unemployed over the long term and this tends to compound the problems in obtaining a job.

It is commonly accepted that the longer someone is unemployed, the more difficult it becomes to get a job. There are many reasons for this. The longer someone is unemployed, the more prospective employers are likely to think they are not a good worker for one reason or another. People who are long-term unemployed are more likely to have few skills, skills that are not in demand from employers, and probably face the severest barriers in finding employment.

Because of this, policy has always placed great emphasis on trying to tackle long-term unemployment. From 1997 until 2001, the United Kingdom experienced a very benign economy with very low unemployment. A combination of labour shortages and government policy has meant that during this time the proportion of the unemployed who are unemployed for a long time has fallen (Figure 6.5). In London, the proportion of unemployed who have been out of work for over one year has almost halved from around 45 per cent in early 1997 to less than 25 per cent in 2001.

Figure 6.5 also shows that the proportion of long-term unemployed in London has moved closer to that in the United Kingdom and South East, although there remains a significant and persistent gap. The data also

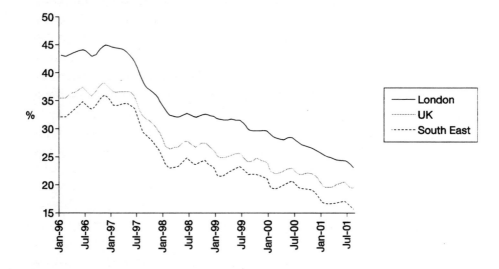

Source: NOMIS (claimant count)

Figure 6.5 Proportion of unemployed who have been unemployed for over one year

mirror the general trends observed in pervious paragraphs – namely, that long-term unemployment in London is less responsive to seasonal forces than it is in the South East.

Youth unemployment

Youth unemployment is another category of the unemployed which has special significance. Young people graduating from school, college and university represent the future. Their first experience, or lack of it, of work can profoundly affect the rest of thcir lives. It is natural that the government is concerned that young people should have the best skills and job opportunities that are within their ability.

Figure 6.6 shows the proportion of unemployed who are aged 18–24 and have been over six months without work. The six-month threshold is significant in two ways. For university graduates and other groups, six months represents a watershed. Many young people may, for example, take a long summer holiday or another form of break after training, but if they are still unemployed after six months this usually means that they have some kind of problem in moving into employment. Six months is also for related reasons the starting point for the government's New Deal programme that began in 1997.

Independent assessment of the New Deal programme by the Institute of Employment Research at the University of Warwick has suggested that the New Deal has indeed contributed significantly to reducing youth unemployment to a level lower than it would have been solely on the basis of improvements in the economy since 1997.

It can be seen from Figure 6.6 that youth unemployment in London follows trends in the United Kingdom more closely than long-term unemployment (Figure 6.5). A slight element of seasonality is noticeable. In the summer months, London tends to have a higher proportion of six months-plus youth unemployment than the United Kingdom, whereas the United Kingdom has a higher proportion in the first quarter of the year. This can probably be explained by the large student population in London who add significantly to the unemployed after graduation each summer. However, the figures show that the proportion of six months-plus youth unemployment in London has consistently deteriorated compared to the South East region. In 1996, youth unemployment in

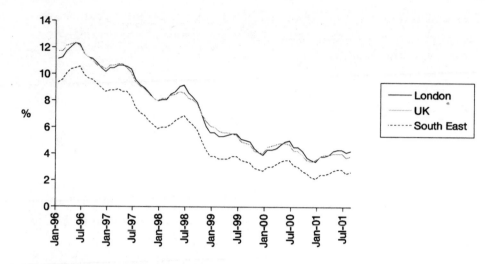

Source: NOMIS (claimant count)

Figure 6.6 Proportion of unemployed aged 18–24 and out of work for six months or more, 1996–2001

London was some 20 per cent higher as a proportion of all unemployment than in the South East. By 2001, it was 60 per cent higher.

It can also be seen that the rate of decline in youth unemployment slows at around 4 per cent of all unemployment. This last 4 per cent of longer-term youth unemployment is likely to be those youths who have the most severe problems – few skills, social difficulties – or who face other barriers in accessing employment. Economists frequently debate the degree to which it is possible to eradicate unemployment altogether or whether there is a 'natural' level below which it will not easily fall. An alternative view of this 4 per cent barrier would be to say that the labour market is beginning to turn and the economic outlook is less favourable, and thus unemployment may start to rise in the future.

Economic activity

A person is economically active when they are taking part in the labour market, which means they are employed, self-employed or seeking work. People who are economically 'inactive' are those who are not seeking work because:

- a disability or long-term illness prevents them from working;
- they are unable to work because of family commitments, including caring for sick relatives;
- they are not interested in looking for a job because they are very wealthy, or they believe they will not be offered a job (the latter are described as 'discouraged workers');
- they are retired, and do not want to work, are full-time students, or are too young to work.

An economic activity rate is the number of economically active as a percentage of the working-age population. It can indicate whether Londoners are becoming more or less likely to participate in the labour market by working or looking for jobs. Both nationally and regionally, men have become less likely to participate in the labour market whereas women have become more likely (Table 6.3). The decline in male participation rates, especially in London, has been associated with the fall in manufacturing and other traditional industries as outlined in Chapter 2. The rise in the proportion of women in the labour market has been influenced by both political change (growing equality) and economic forces which have increased the need for two incomes per household.

Men who used to work in manufacturing have found it difficult to find further employment, as their skills may not have been suitable for employment in the service sector. In the mid-1990s, about half of all the long-term unemployed in London were men who used to work in manufacturing. This dislocation has thus contributed to the persistence of unemployment in the capital. Furthermore, long periods of unemployment have also led to men feeling disillusioned with the labour market and becoming economically inactive. This movement has sometimes added further pressure on women to seek employment.

Table 6.3 indicates that since 1990 economic activity rates for Londoners have been lower than in the United Kingdom as a whole. This is partly a reflection of the changing industrial structure in London, partly a result of the structural unemployment issues discussed in the previous section, and partly a result of the higher barriers to employment in London, such as the high costs of transport and child care.

Table 6.3 Economic activity rates for London

	London			United Kingdom		
	Males	*Females*	*All persons*	*Males*	*Females*	*All persons*
1989	88.4	70.9	79.9	88.3	70.9	80.0
1990	88.7	71.9	80.6	88.3	71.3	80.2
1991	86.7	70.6	78.9	87.7	71.0	79.8
1992	85.5	68.6	77.3	86.3	70.6	78.8
1993	85.9	69.6	78.0	85.6	70.6	78.4
1994	84.3	68.2	76.5	85.2	70.6	78.2
1995	84.1	68.6	76.6	84.7	70.6	78.0
1996	83.9	69.8	77.1	84.6	71.1	78.1
1997	84.6	70.4	77.7	84.4	71.4	78.2
1998	82.6	69.3	76.1	83.9	71.5	78.0
1999	84.2	70.2	77.5	84.1	72.1	78.4
2000	82.9	69.6	76.5	84.8	73.0	78.8
2001	82.6	68.0	75.7	84.2	72.9	78.8

Note: Percentage of the household population of working age (males aged 16–64 and females aged 16–59) who are in the labour force at spring each year
Source: Labour Force Survey, Office for National Statistics

An alternative route into the labour market is self-employment and it is significant that during the 1990s the level of self-employment in London has risen much faster than in the United Kingdom as a whole. Since 1993, the numbers of self-employed in London have risen by over 10 per cent, compared with less than 5 per cent in the country as a whole. Self-employment in London remains a minority form of employment with less than 15 per cent of all those working choosing this route. Numbers of self-employed tend to rise during times of prosperity and fall during a recession as companies cut back on subcontractors. The higher level of self-employment in London reflects the agglomeration effects of a large city, and can be closely linked to entrepreneurialism and the high rate of business formation discussed in Chapter 1.

Deprivation and social exclusion: changing conceptions of disadvantage

Throughout this book, references will be found to 'deprivation' and 'social exclusion' – two key concepts for understanding approaches to unemployment and labour market participation.

The term 'deprivation' has a relatively straightforward definition applying to people who cannot obtain services that they need or want, but is normally applied by public agencies in a more technical sense. The definition used by these agencies is driven by two particular conceptions. First, 'multiple deprivation', the idea that when unemployment, poor housing and social problems are experienced together their combined effects are much worse. Second, there is the idea that such 'multiple deprivation' is concentrated in particular geographic locations. It is thus well known which London boroughs or wards are 'most deprived'. Policies to tackle deprivation have thus tended to be 'area-based policies' that apply to a whole area, to everyone in a ward rather than to people who suffer from particular problems wherever they live.

The main tool for identifying 'areas of deprivation' has been an Index of Deprivation, which is designed to identify the areas in Britain that suffer most, so that they can be targeted as a priority for central government funding. In most of these indices, drawn up since the 1970s, London boroughs have featured prominently as areas of 'high deprivation', their ranking depending to some degree on how the Index has been put together. The indices have been formed by combining different factors relating to poverty and deprivation such as unemployment and infant mortality. The Index used in 2001, whose rankings are mentioned in several tables in this book, is the most complex so far. London boroughs have not been classified as so 'deprived' as in earlier indices, which has led some to question the degree to which the Index reflects the huge problems that are faced in some parts of London. This is not the place to enter a complex debate on this issue. The boroughs that have the most problems emerge clearly in this book, and it has gone some way to explaining both economic aspects of deprivation and some of the reasons for its persistence.

The concept of 'social exclusion' has been a more recent policy development that was first adopted by the European Commission. The EC used this concept to cover those groups of people who had become 'disillusioned' or 'disenfranchised' from society. Deprivation tends to be closely related to unemployment and poverty. In contrast, social exclusion implies a group that is unable to participate in normal social activity. For example, a homeless person has difficulty in holding a bank account (even if they have money), because they do not have an address, and can be excluded from local services because without an address they are not classed as a resident of the area.

In the late 1990s, the concept of social exclusion was taken up in Britain. It is, however, sometimes given a more general definition akin to deprivation. It has, for example, become common to refer to 'economic exclusion' as exclusion from employment.

Both deprivation and social exclusion have become very common terms for describing poor or regeneration areas, in addition to the people who live there. When using them, we must, however, be very clear what problems (and whose problems) we are referring to, in order to be clear how such problems can be addressed.

Population change

The population of London reached a high of 8.6 million in 1939, but then fell over the next 44 years to a low of 6.8 million in 1983. Since then it has steadily increased, but at around 7.2 million in 2001 it has still not reached the level of the early 1970s. Growth during the 1980s, at a time when the cyclical economic forces meant that employment opportunities – particularly for those with lower qualifications – were deteriorating, exacerbated employment problems and added to the level of unemployment.

Much of London's population growth has been among ethnic minority groups who face well-documented barriers to obtaining employment. Research by the London Skills Forecasting Unit (LSFU) in the later 1990s has demonstrated that minorities have twice the level of unemployment as the white population, for the same level of qualification.

Ethnic minority unemployment

The London Skills Survey asks respondents whether they would describe themselves as 'unemployed'. This is a much wider definition than official classifications such as the 'claimant count' (benefits claimants) or the Labour Force Survey ILO definition (whether they have looked for/were available for work in the last four weeks). Nevertheless, the vast majority of unemployed people (80 per cent) had looked for jobs in the last four weeks, and similar levels of job search were recorded for unemployed people from different ethnic minorities.

When the unemployed and the inactive were asked why they were not seeking work, white respondents were more likely to state that it was due to family commitments and poor health or illness (Table 6.4). The other remaining ethnic groups were more likely to state that they were still in education.

Unemployed people from ethnic minorities were more likely than those from white groups to say that they would be looking for work (Table 6.5). Some people may have to find work quickly because of low incomes, others may have been involved in a succession of short-term jobs, as implied by the analysis of the duration of unemployment (Table 6.6).

The 1998 London Skills Survey suggested that although people from ethnic minorities tended to have higher rates of unemployment than white people, they tended also to spend a shorter time without a job. Table 6.6 shows that this remained the case in 1999 despite the overall fall in the number of unemployed and the fall in the average duration of joblessness in the whole workforce. There has been a remarkably large fall in the duration of unemployment among Bangladeshi people, and a remarkably small decrease in unemployment duration among Black Caribbean people. Some of these changes may be explained by differences in sampling, but the overall trend both between years and between ethnic groups is consistent.

Table 6.4 Main reason for not actively seeking work at the moment

	All	White	Mixed	Asian/ Asian British	Black/ black British	Chinese	Other
	%	%	%	% %	%	%	
Still in education	39	33	47	66	57	70	52
Family commitments	36	39	33	16	27	22	34
In poor health/ill/disabled	13	15	7	7	7	5	7
No suitable jobs available	1	1	–	2	*	–	*
Retired	2	3	1	1	*	–	2
No need to work	1	1	–	–	*	–	*
Just left previous job	1	1	–	1	*	–	–
Age/too old	2	2	1	1	*	–	–
Given up trying/feel discouraged	*	*	1	*	1	–	–
Other	4	4	2	4	6	4	5
Not stated	2	2	7	3	1	–	–
Total	3,170	2,378	94	257	308	30	65

Source: London Skills Survey, 1999
Note: * = less than 1
      – = 0
All inactive/unemployed respondents who have not looked for work in the last four weeks

Table 6.5 Whether likely to look for work in the next 12 months by economic situation, age, sex and ethnicity

	Yes	No	N/S	Base
	%	%	%	*N*
All	30	59	11	3,170
Economic activity				
Unemployed	66	24	10	159
Inactive	28	61	11	3,011
Ethnicity				
White	28	61	11	2,378
Mixed race	35	52	13	94
Asian/Asian British	30	56	14	257
Black/black British	38	50	12	308
Chinese	27	55	18	30
Other	29	57	14	65

Source: London Skills Survey, 1999
Note: All inactive and unemployed respondents who have not looked for work in the last four weeks

Table 6.6 Average length of unemployment (months) by ethnicity

Ethnic Group	1998	1999	Change	Percentage change
White	19.9	15.3	−4.6	−23.1
Irish		15.9		
Indian	13.0	9.3	−3.7	−28.5
Bangladeshi	20.5	8.0	−12.5	−61.0
Pakistani	11.0	8.0	−3.0	−27.3
Black African	14.5	10.5	−4.0	−27.6
Black Caribbean	17.3	16.3	−1.0	−5.7
All unemployed	18.9	13.8	−5.1	−27.0

Source: London Skills Survey, 1999

The interpretation of these results is unclear. It may be that unemployed people from ethnic minorities are more frequently unemployed, but for shorter periods of time, or that the jobs they acquire are short-term and informal positions within their own communities as suggested by data in the Employer Survey discussed above. The survey evidence of highly qualified unemployed in ethnic minority groups certainly supports a more negative interpretation of employment prospects.

Dependency and worklessness

Since the mid-1990s, there has been a great concern about the growing number of people nationally who are out of work but who do not feature in unemployment lists either because they are not eligible for unemployment benefits or because they do not meet standard definitions of the unemployed. For example, a trend has been identified for the growth of 'workless households'. It has been argued that during the mid-1990s as the United Kingdom moved out of recession, job growth tended to be concentrated in households where there was already an earner.[3] This can be linked to the increasing participation of women in the labour market, but more worrying was the tendency alongside this for an increase in households with no earner. London and other metropolitan areas have suffered most from this trend. In 1979, less than 10 per cent of Inner London households had no one in work. By 1996, this had risen to almost 25 per cent.[4]

These trends have also been accompanied by a rise in the numbers of people, and households, on forms of benefit other than unemployment. Table 6.7 presents figures for London for some major types of benefit for the same boroughs discussed in Chapter 2. As in the case of Table 2.5, the degree of polarisation is clear. The extent of the problem in 1999 was also apparent, when just under half of all the children living in Hackney lived in families dependent on Income Support. As in the previous discussion of the distribution of deprivation in London, some of the anomalies also become apparent. For example, although relatively prosperous, the Borough of Hillingdon contains a high proportion of children on Income Support. These children may well be from large ethnic minority households and associated with areas of high deprivation in the otherwise prosperous western part of London, such as the Park Royal estate.

Regional analysis suggests that the overall level of benefit dependency indicated by these figures is similar to other metropolitan areas.[5] The polarisation is perhaps more extreme in London. The level of Incapacity

---

[3] For example, by the Centre for Economic Performance of the London School of Economics, and Paul Gregg.

[4] Llewelyn-Davies, UCL Bartlett School of Planning, University of Reading, and University of Essex, *The London Study: a socio-economic assessment of London*, Association of London Government (1997), p 43.

[5] London Research Centre, Office for National Statistics, and Government Office for London, *Focus on London 2000* (2000), pp 92–4.

Table 6.7 Numbers receiving social benefits in London, 1999

	% of those aged 16–59 receiving Incapacity Benefit*	% of those aged 16–59 receiving Income Support#	% of population under 16 living in hhlds with Income Support*	% of population under 16 living in hhlds with Family Credit§	Deprivation rank 2000, average rank of wards, 1 is most deprived
Some of the most prosperous boroughs					
City of London	5	9	10	5	205
Westminster	4	11	25	7	141
Hillingdon	4	9	19	6	201
Kingston	3	6	10	4	318
Richmond	3	5	9	3	341
Sutton	4	7	13	5	254
Some boroughs most in need of regeneration					
Southwark	8	18	34	9	9
Islington	9	19	37	8	8
Haringey	7	18	36	8	37
Newham	9	22	37	13	3
Hackney	10	24	40	14	2
Tower Hamlets	10	22	37	18	1

Source: Department for Work & Pensions Information Centre (Analytical Services Division), and Office for National Statistics
Notes:
* Incapacity Benefit supports those who cannot work because of long-term illness or disability
\# Income Support is long-term support for those who are not required to be available for work
§ Family Credit is financial support for families on low incomes with young children

Benefit in London has, for example, proved to be generally lower than in other metropolitan areas but, as can be seen, the poorer boroughs still have over twice the claimants.

Other Londoners facing particular barriers to employment[6]

This chapter has outlined the problems faced by the unemployed and some specific groups among them – ethnic minorities and those suffering

---

6   Information in this section derives from LSFU, *Creating the Learning Capital* (2001).

from 'multiple deprivation' or 'social exclusion'. There are also a number of other groups that face particular problems when trying to enter the London labour market.

We have pointed out how women in London have begun to be far more active in the labour market, in common with those in other parts of the United Kingdom. However, they face many more barriers in working in London than in other areas. Child care and transport costs are higher in London, making the financial barrier to employment (the level at which taking a job becomes financially viable) significantly higher than in other parts of the United Kingdom. The high wages in many London companies attract the leading businesswomen, but at the lower end of the labour market low wages in part-time jobs can be a significant problem for women who would like to work.

LSFU research has identified significant barriers to employment among the over-50s, an age group for whom the government is seeking to widen employment opportunities. Over-50s in London are more likely to be working than in other parts of the country, reflecting perhaps both the high level of senior managers in London company HQs and significant levels of poverty which oblige older people to carry on working. However, over-50s were more likely than other age groups to have no qualifications and to have been unemployed for over two years.

The disabled face many problems in trying to obtain employment. These problems include misperceptions about their mental capability as well as the more obvious difficulties of access for those with physical disabilities. Research by LSFU suggests that disabled people in London are less likely to be involved in training and less likely to be interested in training than their able-bodied counterparts. This suggests that public agencies not only need to encourage employers and trainers to take on disabled people, but also need to work more with disabled people to explain to them how they can access opportunities for both training and employment.

These brief paragraphs could be duplicated for many other groups who live in London and who are discouraged by barriers to employment. They serve to illustrate the severe hardships faced by some Londoners. It is important to understand how a variety of different factors can combine to cause real hardship that can create persistent long-term difficulties in finding work. This chapter has done no more than touch the surface of some of these problems and they underline the fact that London's great wealth and resources need to be deployed to help the many disadvantaged people in the capital.

Conclusion

This chapter has attempted to look at a number of the structural issues that lie behind unemployment in London. At the beginning of the chapter it was suggested that unemployment in London tends to rise faster than in other regions when the national economy worsens. This is partly because of the kinds of jobs that there are in London (administrative jobs), partly because of the concentration among London residents of vulnerable groups of employed (low-skilled) and partly because of economic effects such as the number of small contractors whose contracts can be cut back.

Equally, London's unemployment rate has been shown to be slow to recover from recession. New jobs have tended to be taken by other members of working households (as opposed to those without a wage earner), there has been competition for jobs from people outside London, and the new jobs may not be the same type of jobs as those that were lost (shift from manufacturing to services). Thus, if London does not have enough time to recover before the next downturn, unemployment will tend to rise over the longer term as compared to South East England.

The second half of this chapter outlined some of the problems surrounding unemployment by exploring the concepts of deprivation and exclusion. It has been noted that London has concentrations of groups that are particularly subject to such problems, including ethnic minorities, workless households and the disabled. Both Chapter 5 and this chapter have discussed some of the difficulties that such groups can face in breaking out of the cycle of deprivation.

The picture is therefore one in which economic cycles, the structure of the London economy and the depth or complexity of the problems faced by some groups conspire together to make unemployment in London particularly intractable and persistent. Against this somewhat gloomy viewpoint we must set the commitment of so many public agencies, community groups and the unemployed themselves to find meaningful jobs. The struggle against unemployment and exclusion is the most critical one facing London today. This chapter has been written very much in the spirit of it being important 'to know what we are up against'.

7

The Future

London is a world leader, an attractive place in which people across the United Kingdom and the world want to live and work. However, it suffers from congestion and high costs of living partly because of its attractiveness and relative success. It takes pride in innovation and diversity. London's achievements in music, in architecture and in business can be breathtaking. When Londoners pull together, the earth moves. It is often said that individuals can feel isolated in a big city, but the depth of community feeling in London, from neighbourhood solidarity to business networks, can provide an overwhelming sense of vitality and belonging.

This book has focused on the longer-term factors that have influenced the London economy and labour market. It has suggested a number of key dimensions in which London is changing and some others in which London is not changing (or is changing very slowly). The intention of this chapter is to consider, within these limits, what the future may hold for the British capital city.

Sectoral shifts

Chapter 1 highlighted the importance of certain sectors in London and the long-term shift of employment from manufacturing to services. Financial and business services remain at the heart of the London economy. In the case of finance, it was suggested that the City was not only based on London's position as a global market maker, but was inextricably linked to a broader base of services in the UK market. Thus, London does rely on a broad economic base. In the case of business services, it was suggested that London's ability to compete relies on the creativity of its workers and citizens.

The most recent development in services has been related to the increasing sophistication of ICT, allowing tailoring of 'informational' products to a variety of customers, and the instant distribution of such products over the Internet. Growth in the 1990s also suggested that ICT is beginning to contribute directly to competitiveness through increased productivity.

In the future, this shift is likely to continue, with further changes in the service sector. Business services, particularly small businesses producing specialised products, will change their market focus, creating new groupings and services. The 1990s have seen the emergence of the New Media sector and mergers between the major companies in newspapers, television and Internet. In the future, one might, for example, see the development of a grouping specialising in service delivery by mobile phone.

These changes are, in effect, creating new service sub-sectors as businesses find new alliances and new ways of providing integrated services to customers. It may be expected that in another 20 years the business service sector may have a very different complexion with different groupings of companies that we would find hard to recognise today.

Another major change has been the increasing use of prefabrication or pre-preparation of products such as food or construction components. These movements are also likely to become more sophisticated. In construction, handheld computers/phones may be used for specifying prefabricated modules on site. This change has had a profound effect on production and manufacturing. Intensification of this process can be expected in hand with aspects of globalisation/localisation.

Globalisation has been engendered by a realisation that although components of, say, a car can be produced anywhere in the world, consumers appreciate products which have branding and identity appropriate for their country, and indeed a product which is unique in their neighbourhood. The car industry and the IT industry, in particular, have placed great emphasis on global production systems, which can respond to the requests of individual customers with regard to items such as styling, colour and components (eg cars: music systems; IT: screen size). In the future, one can expect more responsiveness to individuals' requirements, but also more remote production.

Ethnic minority businesses will play an increasingly important part in London. The rise in ethnic minority groups means that their communities will become more significant markets for London products. All Londoners will benefit more and more from the increasing diversity of products and services produced by these groups. The cultural richness of London will grow, increasing creativity further.

In this regard, the hospitality sector is the most critical for the London economy. It includes something like half of all ethnic-minority-owned businesses. It provides the first job for the majority of school leavers and students. If young people have a bad experience of work in this sector, it may well influence their attitude to work in general. Furthermore, the ethnic minority population of London is young and expanding. Problems in this sector, including the recent slump in tourist numbers, could quickly translate into higher unemployment and exclusion.

However, rather then being too pessimistic we should remain confident that the diversity and entrepreneurialism in London's small businesses, built on its creativity, will always be developing new ideas and products and maintaining London's pre-eminent role in the world economy.

Geographical shifts and the changing nature of work

Perhaps the two greatest geographical shifts that have taken place in the last 20 years in London are those on its western and eastern edges – the development of the M4 corridor and the redevelopment of the Docklands. While East London will continue to make marked strides in this respect, it is hard to see changes on a similar scale in the near future.

Developments in East London have led to the possibility of an eastern corridor between London and Cambridge, linking the new financial districts with the technological innovation of Cambridge.

The changing nature of work has been a subject for much discussion at various times during the 1980s and 1990s. It was first concerned with flexible working, involving increases in contract working, temporary working and flexible hours. This formulation has been more recently revised as the 'portfolio' worker, a worker who has a variety of business interests and skills. This has given rise to the importance of trainability – the readiness of people with academic and vocational qualifications to 'fit in' with their new jobs quickly and engage in production efficiently.

It is true that, at times during the 1980s and 1990s, the number of contractors and temporary workers has increased tremendously, but they still represent a small proportion of the overall labour market. Thus, it is unlikely that the majority of workers will be employed under such arrangements in the future.

Chapter 4 drew attention to the competition for work between residents of London and commuters, particularly at NVQ Level 3 and above. It is hard to see how this degree of competition might be reduced – indeed, it is most likely to become more intense. Globalisation, easier travel (at regional, national and international levels) and freer European labour markets are all likely to increase the flow of non-London residents into London. However, one can expect this demand to be offset by continuing rises in London house prices to meet demand from all of these groups. This scenario would then see a continuing need for affordable housing for key workers and those on low pay.

When discussing unemployment, we noted how London reacts quickly to a downturn and is slower to recover in periods of prosperity than the adjacent South East. This was linked to the ability of commuters in the South East to compete for jobs. If, as suggested in the previous paragraph, this competition were to intensify, London's position may deteriorate compared to that of the South East.

The opportunities to acquire great wealth in a big city are a major reason for both those with high-level skills to migrate to the city and those with low-level skills to come here. The wealth created by those who are successful in some part goes to compensate for unemployment among those who are not successful. It has been suggested that when people living in areas of high unemployment obtain a job, they move out of 'deprived' areas to be replaced by more poor or disadvantaged people. Just as commuters travelling from the South East to jobs in London maintain the low level of unemployment in that region, so new low-skilled or unemployed people moving onto disadvantaged council estates tend to maintain the high level of unemployment in these areas.

It is unclear how these cycles can be broken. This is the most pessimistic part of the book, but the facts are unavoidable. A wide variety of initiatives are needed to address the prolonged problems of unemployment and exclusion. The later chapters of this book have detailed something of how hard such problems can be. London's attractiveness to people from all walks of life has its advantages and disadvantages.

This is not to say that regeneration has failed London. An enormous range of regeneration projects has helped huge numbers of people over a long period of time. Some people may have missed out on opportunities or been caught up again in poverty and exclusion, but many others have been helped to obtain a sustainable job and a better life. The point is more that those who are successful tend to leave, to be replaced by other people who need the help of public agencies to gain employment.

Changes in the nature of learning

The studies of international competitiveness in Chapter 3 outlined how companies working in London saw the skills of the local workforce as the most important contributor to their competitiveness. Later chapters reinforced this judgement by indicating how critical skills are in obtaining work.

The talents of both the 'low'- and 'high'-skilled worker are critical for London. The daily life of London is driven by many frontline customer service staff in all kinds of businesses who help to create the image of London in the way in which they deal with customers and help visitors. This is just as important a contribution as the highly skilled workers and business leaders who drive forward their companies and innovate, thus maintaining London's competitiveness. Working in the City one is struck by the night-time population of cleaners and support staff who keep the centre of world finance going when the dealers are not in their offices.

High technology, research and development and ICT will all be increasingly important in the future to maintain London's competitive edge, but as this book has made clear, such functions do not operate in isolation. Service industries and support staff are also vital to make London work and to attract innovators to live and work in the city. We have deliberately not discussed the physical environment in this book; much has been written on this and can be read elsewhere. Suffice to say here that without the people who create and look after this infrastructure, at all levels from public service managers to cleaners, nurses, teachers, bus and train drivers, innovators (and everybody else!) would be much less interested in living or working in London.

It is thus going to be as important to train the low skilled as it is to improve the competencies of the high skilled. London's future depends on both. Globalisation increasingly means that the same products can be produced anywhere. London's future depends on quality more than price, as there will always be places in the Third World that can produce cheaper products. In the future, levels of service will become increasingly critical and it is those levels and quality of service, as much as financial rewards, which will attract the highly skilled professionals and innovators that London's businesses need to remain truly groundbreaking.

Chapter 5 drew attention to the distinction between qualifications and skills. Qualifications are like a coin whose value is judged by those who use them (both students and employers). A qualification allows employers and prospective employees to come to an agreement about the overall level of their knowledge. By contrast, people find it difficult to come to a common understanding about the level of a person's skills unless they have personal knowledge of them when they use that skill. In general, the world of educationalists and trainers has moved towards more of an interest in skills, and with this has come a wider appreciation of the value in different forms of learning. Two kinds of learning are significant here: informal learning and e-learning.

Informal learning is the learning that takes place when a person is informally shown how to do something, or learning through self-tuition when one simply decides to read a book on 'How to...'. In the work place, it can be associated with mentoring or supervision. There is increasing interest in capturing how much this goes on and how much it contributes to overall skills development. In the future, therefore, informal learning may become more institutionalised as a way of encouraging people to acquire new skills. From the point of view of the London economy this means that there will be new attempts to harness informal learning to enhance London's competitiveness. Informal learning is very well suited to developing the quality of service that London needs to compete.

E-learning is learning over the Internet. It allows people to access learning, from their desks, on demand at any time of the day. It can lead to formal qualifications. It can also take place in a very informal setting. Many large companies have used e-learning to institute in-house training programmes. Companies have bypassed formal qualification routes by using e-learning and other forms of in-house training. The government has set up Learning Direct to allow individuals to gain access to a wide range of such learning opportunities.

E-learning is complementary to informal learning. Interactive tests allow the self-taught to test themselves and gain accredited qualifications. The very flexibility of e-learning suggests that it will receive widespread take-up in the future (except among those groups that are IT-excluded). E-learning and informal learning tend to take learning out of the class-room and into the work place in a flexible form that allows it to be under-taken on the job. Thus, the future may well see less classroom-based training, a wider range of e-qualifications and less traditional exam-based qualifications.

The more flexible nature of learning and training provision is some-thing to which formal educational institutions at all levels will need to respond. Colleges and universities are beginning to find, and will increas-ingly need to find, ways of reaching out into the work place and the community in order to deliver learning when and how businesses and individual students want it. Many people, particularly those without access to IT, will still prefer a conventional classroom; others will require learning at their desk or at home, in short bursts when time allows them to pursue it.

This does not mean the abandonment of qualifications that will keep their vital role as a currency of exchange between different people, allow-ing them to compare their level of knowledge with others and validating their learning achievement with a certificate.

This further flexibility of learning is particularly important for London, where quality of service is such an important element of its competitive-ness. The London labour market allows frequent changes of employment. Companies restructure frequently and there is a rapid turnover in the number of small businesses. Qualifications help in establishing some benchmarks in this volatile labour market, and the quality of work that a worker demonstrates can be a decisive factor for employers choosing between workers with similar qualifications.[1]

The London Skills Forecasting Unit (LSFU) has been concerned to examine the relationship between companies that adopt a proactive up-skilling strategy and successful growth through productivity and

---

[1]   M Spilsbury and K Lane, *Skills Needs and Recruitment Practices in Central London*, Focus Central London (2000).

innovation.[2] There is considerable academic debate on this point, which is too complex to repeat here. Suffice to say that it is difficult to prove whether training leads to growth or whether growth leads to an increase in training provision. However, given the significant contribution to the London economy that skills have been said to play in several chapters of this book, the results of the debate are likely to be important to the development of the capital.

The overall aim of London must be to raise the quality of skills at all levels while raising the level of qualifications in the workforce. London is already ahead of other regions in its levels of qualification – it must and will stay there. Those with low or no qualifications must be encouraged to train and stretch their capabilities.

Business cycle – 'boom and bust?'

Many people are now familiar with the picture of the United Kingdom in the 1970s and 1980s as a 'boom and bust' economy. Periods of prosperity resulting in over-optimism, over-spending and high-priced housing were followed by a crash into recession and high unemployment. At the end of the 1990s, unprecedented world prosperity and a more cautious approach to managing the UK economy seemed to suggest that this cyclical volatility was over.

In 2001 and 2002, people are much less certain. An economic slowdown, BSE, foot-and-mouth and terrorism have all demonstrated that the economy is still subject to a wide range of shocks. A downturn is likely, if not already in evidence.

Unemployment, which has, after all, been at its lowest for over 20 years, is more likely to go up than down. Many, if not most, economists believe that the downturn will not be too severe, since governments have learnt the lessons of earlier cycles and are much more cautious in their actions.

London, as has been indicated in this book, is likely to feel the recession before other regions of the United Kingdom. In the late 1990s, the newspaper headlines were full of 'skills shortages' and the ICT revolution. It is

---

[2]   S Ellis, 'Anticipating employer skills needs', *International Journal of Manpower Planning* (forthcoming), and *idem*, *Proceedings of Regional Studies Conference 1999*.

likely that they will again turn to the need to reduce unemployment and create jobs. We will have to rely on the competitiveness of London's businesses and the tireless work of London's myriad public and community agencies to keep as many people as possible in employment. It is impossible to know how long such downturns might last, but again it should be shorter and less severe than previous periods of recession. It is even possible that the majority of London workers will not notice any difference in their lives.

The experiences of 2001 have shown that the business cycle, economic downturns and economic shocks are one of the unavoidable ugly realities of life. Governments and other agencies intervene to alleviate such problems, but they cannot be avoided altogether.

We know, nonetheless, that we can rely on the creativity of Londoners and on the resilience of London's key industrial sectors and companies to carry London through the hard times and back onto the road of economic expansion, well into the 21st century.

'Polarisation'

Throughout this work a contrast has been drawn between rich and poor, high skills and low skilled, employed and unemployed. It is often said that the skyscrapers of the City and Canary Wharf nestle near to some of the poorest areas of Europe. This book has suggested that those with high skills tend to learn more while the unemployed do not. Those on high incomes are better able to migrate, both short and long distances, to find work and achieve a better quality of life. The poor can find it very hard to leave their estates.

Some consider that the future of London holds a 'polarisation' of London's workers. Chapter 5, for example, has highlighted the 'intermediate' skills problem. As the highly skilled gain more skills, they can leave the unskilled further behind. The 'digital divide' can isolate those with no IT skills. It is likely that the picture is much more complicated than this. Often, what people lack in one dimension they make up for in another – instead of technical IT knowledge, they have entrepreneurial skills or creativity. Chapter 5 has also suggested, in line with some recent forecasts, that the future does hold increased demand for low-skilled as well as high-skilled workers.

Academic research[3] has suggested that qualifications in Britain and the United States are distributed very unevenly – at degree level and above, and at low qualifications with proportionately few people at intermediate levels – compared to other European countries. This has also been associated with a British economy that competes with low-quality products, requiring a low-qualified workforce. Information presented in Chapter 5 (Tables 5.2 and 5.21) suggests that London may have a more even spread of qualifications in its workforce than other regions of the United Kingdom.

Most important is the need to avoid 'polarisation' of attitudes towards the unemployed and the low skilled, to avoid discrimination by ethnicity or 'postcode'.

The people of London will work together to help those that suffer from deprivation and exclusion, and to create the wealth that will create sustainable jobs at all levels into the future.

---

[3] See A Green and H Steedman, *Into the Twenty First Century: an assessment of British skill profiles and prospects*, CEP London School of Economics (1997), and P Brown, A Green and H Lauder, *High Skills, Globalization, Competitiveness and Skill Formation*, Oxford (2001).

Glossary

ABI – Annual Business Inquiry The main annual source of company data, linked to government departments' Inter-Departmental Business Register (IDBR). Used as the main basis for sectoral breakdowns per local authority area by employment and number of companies. Until the 1990s, data were gathered through the Census of Employment.

Business Cycle The theory of the business cycle predicts a series of alternating periods of prosperity and recession. For example, in prosperous times prices rise, then consumer demand may fall, leading to reduced profits, redundancies, high unemployment and cheap labour. Cheap labour can lead to reduced costs, bigger profits and so to prosperity. Economists have identified several different business cycles of different numbers of years. The degree to which these business cycles interact may increase the 'boom' or lead to a 'bust'.

Deprivation, Index of Deprivation is usually shorthand for 'multiple deprivation' which identifies areas that suffer from a complex mixture of disadvantages including high unemployment, health risks, social problems and a poor environment. The government has constructed the Index of Deprivation to provide an overall ranking of the most 'deprived' areas in the country. Deprivation has become close to social exclusion in meaning.

Economically Active This term is used to describe people who are 'active' in the labour market – in other words, people who are employed, self-employed or unemployed. The unemployed are 'active' as they are looking for jobs and form part of the overall labour pool from which employers hire workers. The 'inactive' are not part of the labour market – in other words, they are not seeking jobs because they are either retired, full-time students, suffer from a disability preventing them from working, have a 'carer' role that prevents them from working, or simply do not want to work.

GDP – Gross Domestic Product Value in £s of production, usually of a country or perhaps a region. Can be assessed i) per head of resident population, or ii) per member of workforce. Resident estimates for London are much higher than workforce, as the former do not take into account commuters.

LFS – Labour Force Survey The national survey of workers, the unemployed and inactive, based on a sample of households. Generally accurate down to local authority areas, but many very defined variables with small samples (eg specific ethnic minorities with a particular qualification) may only be accurate at regional level. Consistent with other national labour force surveys in Europe, allowing some European comparisons. www.statistics.gov.uk

NUTS – Nomenclature of Territorial Statistics An area classification used by the European Union to provide a comparable level of geographic coverage across Europe. NUTS 1 is regions including London, NUTS 2 is Inner and Outer London, NUTS 4 is local authorities including London boroughs.

NVQ – National Vocational Qualification NVQs are a set of qualifications designed to incorporate and validate experience gained in work. However, their main significance in this work is that all other UK qualifications have been given an 'NVQ equivalent' which enables the workforce to be profiled by their qualification level. Table 5.1 sets out these equivalents.

Productivity The unit cost of production. In terms of the labour market, it is usually seen as company turnover per worker, although it can be defined in several different ways including turnover per hour of work. British productivity is generally thought to be lower than that of other countries.

SIC – Standard Industrial Classification. This is the system used to classify different companies according to their industrial sector. The last classification of this type, which is used in this book, was released in 1992, and is now being revised. When an official classification, it is written in initial capitals – Hotels and Catering – to distinguish it from an unofficial sectoral description – hospitality.

SOC – Standard Occupational Classification. This is the system used to classify the types of activity carried out by different groups of workers. A revised classification was issued in 2000, and this is normally used in this book, including throughout Chapter 5. As in the case of SIC, initial capitals are used for official occupational categories – managers and senior officials.

Social exclusion A term that has become more common at the end of the 1990s to describe those who no longer have access to a range of public and private services. Can also be phrased as 'social inclusion' to suggest the need to bring all groups back into society. Its meaning has become closely associated with deprivation.

Unemployment rates Unemployment can be measured by the proportion of the workforce who are claiming benefit (known as the claimant count), or the proportion of the workforce who have been looking for a job in the last four weeks (the International Labour Organisation – ILO definition). Numbers of claimants are published each month, but the ILO rate is measured quarterly using the Labour Force Survey.

Sources

DfES Skillsbase Statistics site of the Department for Education and Skills. Includes much research carried out in 1998–2000 by the National Skills Taskforce, including occupational and skills projections and results of the national employer and skills surveys. www.skillsbase.dfee.gov.uk

DTI The Statistics Directorate is a source of many economic statistics, including VAT registrations and the important Regional Competitiveness Indicators. www.dti.gov.uk/sd/index.htm

Eurostat Official statistics agency of the European Commission. Most statistics by subscription only, although there are some free downloads. Mostly national and European data, but also includes a good number of reports based on regions within the European Union (see NUTS in Glossary). Europa.eu.int/comm/eurostat/

London Employer Survey Annual survey of 5,000 employers conducted by London Skills Forecasting Unit (LSFU). www.skills-unit.com

London Skills Survey Annual survey of 14,000 individuals (residents and commuters) conducted by LSFU. www.skills-unit.com

NOMIS National On-line Manpower Information System. Run out of the University of Durham. Free access upon registration to a wide range of national labour market statistics. www.nomisweb.co.uk

Office for National Statistics Official agency responsible for national statistics in the United Kingdom. Operates the Labour Force Survey and the national Census of Population. Results of the 2001 Census are expected in late 2002 or early 2003. It also operates the important Neighbourhood Statistics website with wide range of statistics, including much benefits and deprivation data based on local council wards. www.statistics.gov.uk

Bibliography

A wide range of studies on the London economy is published every year. This Bibliography only lists some of the most important studies and those that are referred to directly in the main text.

Ashton, D. et al (2001), *Work Skills in Britain 2000 – SKOPE*.

Bank for International Settlements (2001), *Central Banks Survey*.

Beinart, S. and Smith, P. (1998), *National Adult Learning Survey 1997*, DfEE Research Report 49.

Brauerhjelm, P. et al (2000), *Integration and Regions of Europe: How the right practice can prevent polarisation*, CEPR.

Brown, P., Green, A. and Lauder, H. (2001), *High Skills, Globalization, Competitiveness and Skill Formation*, Oxford.

Centre for Economic and Business Research, Observatoire de l'Economie et des Institutions Locales (1997), *Two Great Cities: a comparison of the economies of London and Paris*, Corporation of London.

Centre for Economic and Business Research (1998), *The City's Importance to the European Union Economy*, Corporation of London.

Centre for Economic and Business Research (1999), *The Competitiveness of London's Financial and Business Services Sector*, Corporation of London.

Centre for Economic and Business Research (2000), *London's Contribution to the UK Economy*, Corporation of London.

Corporation of London (2000), *London–New York Study*, 3 vols.

CRCI Ile-de-France (1999), *Référence Emploi Formation*.

Focus Central London (1999), *Ethnic Minority Businesses in Lambeth and Southwark*.

Focus Central London (1999), *IT Skills Needs and Training Provision in Central London*.

Gordon, I. R. (1999), 'A long-term perspective on inter-regional migration', *Regional Economic Prospects*.

Gordon, I. R. and McCann, P. (2000), 'Industrial clusters: complexes, agglomerations, and/or social networks', *Urban Studies*.

Greater London Authority (2001), *Towards the London Plan*.

Greater London Enterprise and Middlesex University Business School (2000), *Review of Business Support for Ethnic Minority-owned businesses in London*.

Green, A. and Steedman, H. (1997), *Into the Twenty First Century: an assessment of British skill profiles and prospects*, CEP London School of Economics.

Hirsch, F. (1977), *The Social Limits to Growth*, London.

INTER/VIEW (1992), *The Competitive Advantage of Ten Major Cities in Europe*.

Keep, E. and Mayhew, K. (1994), *Training Policy for Competitiveness: time for a fresh perspective*.

Keep, E. and Mayhew, K. (1998), *What makes training pay*, Institute of Personnel and Development.

Laafia, I. (2001), *R&D expenditure and personnel in Europe and its regions*, Eurostat.

Llewelyn-Davies, UCL Bartlett School of Planning, (1996), *Four World Cities: a comparative study of London, Paris, New York and Tokyo*.

Llewelyn-Davies, UCL Bartlett School of Planning, University of Reading and University of Essex (1997), *The London Study: a socio-economic assessment of London*, Association of London Government.

Local Futures Group (1998), *The London Study: a strategic framework for London*, Association of London Government.

Local Futures Group (1998), *Telecommunications and Regional Development – Focus on London*, BT, London.

Local Futures Group (1999), *The Role of the City in London's Knowledge-driven Information Economy*, Corporation of London.

London Business School (1995), *The City Research Project*, Corporation of London.

London Development Agency (2001), *Success through Diversity: London's Economic Development Strategy*.

London Development Partnership (2000), *Building London's Economy*.

London Planning Advisory Committee (1991), *London: World City*.

London Research Centre (1996), *The Capital Divided: mapping poverty and social exclusion in London*, London.

London Research Centre (1997), *London's Workers: from the 1991 Census*, London.

London Research Centre (1997), *Cosmopolitan London: past, present and future*, London.

London Research Centre, Government Office for London, Office for National Statistics (2000), *Focus on London 2000*, HMSO.

London Skills and Forecasting Unit (1999), *London Employer Survey*.

London Skills Forecasting Unit (1999), *London – Understanding the Global City*.

London Skills Forecasting Unit (1999), *Strength through Diversity: ethnic minorities in London's economy*.

London Skills Forecasting Unit (2000), *Second Annual Report*.

London Skills Forecasting Unit (2000), *Skills For Tomorrow's High St.*

London Skills Forecasting Unit (2000), *Creative Skills: skills for London's creative industries in the digital age*.

London Skills Forecasting Unit (2001), *Ethnic Capital: shaping London's local economies*.

London Skills Forecasting Unit (2001), *Third Annual Report*.

London Skills Forecasting Unit (2001), *Creating the Learning Capital: identifying non-learners in London.*

London Skills Forecasting Unit (2001), *Production Skills in the Digital Economy.*

London Skills Forecasting Unit, L'Observatoire de la Formation de l'Emploi et des Métiers (2001), *Les villes apprenantes/Learning Cities.*

London TEC Council (1996), *An Economic Profile of London.*

Londonomics Ltd (2000), *Global Cities Benchmarking: a feasibility study on performance indicators and competitiveness index for London,* London Skills Forecasting Unit.

Londonomics Ltd (2000), *London's Competitiveness Index – Weighting the Indicators,* London Skills Forecasting Unit.

NACETT (1998), *Fast Forward for Skills.*

National Housing Federation (2001), *Mind the Gap: housing London's key workers.*

Porter, M. (1990), *The Competitive Advantage of Nations,* New York.

Pilos, S. (2001), *Education in the Regions of the European Union,* Eurostat.

Richardson, P. et al (2000), 'The concept, policy use and measurement of structural unemployment: estimating a time varying NAIRU across 21 OECD countries', OECD Economics Department Working Papers.

Rogers, A., ed. (1992), *Elderly Migration and Population Redistribution: a comparative study,* London.

Rossi, P. H. (1980), *Why Families Move,* London.

SOSTRA (2000), *Betriebspanel Berlin 1999: Ergebnisse der vierten Welle,* Berlin Senatverwaltung fur Arbeit, Soziales und Frauen.

Spilsbury, M. and Lane, K. (2000), *Skills Needs and Recruitment Practices in Central London,* Focus Central London.

West London TEC (1999), *IT Skills into the Twenty-First Century.*